C000292135

Walking
Glenfinnan

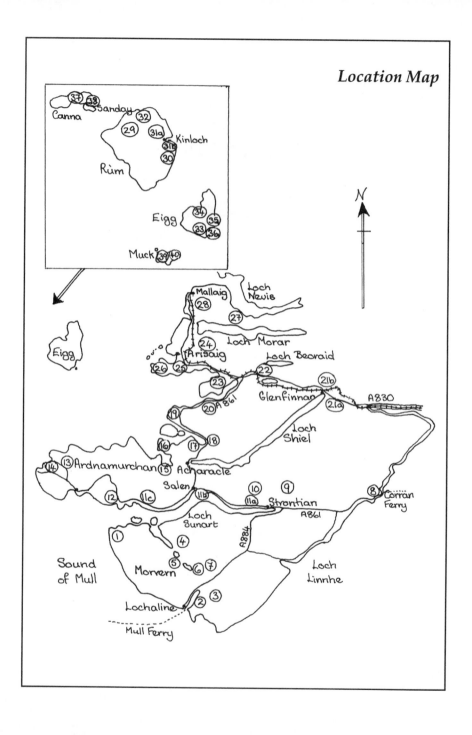

Clan Walk Guides

Walking Glenfinnan

The Road to the Isles

Morar · Ardnamurchan

Moidart · Morvern

The Small Isles

Canna · Rum · Eigg · Muck

Mary Welsh
and
Christine Isherwood

First published by Clan Books, 2007
Incorporating chapters originally published under the title
Walks on Canna, Rum, Eigg and Muck by
Westmorland Gazette, 1996

ISBN 978 1 873597 14 9

Text and Illustrations
© Mary Welsh
and
Christine Isherwood 2007

Clan Books
Clandon House
The Cross, Doune
Perthshire
FK16 6BE

Printed and bound in Great Britain by
St Edmundsbury Press Ltd, Bury St Edmunds, Suffolk

Publisher's Notes

In planning new titles in the Clan Walk Guides series, our main concern has been that each new volume should cover an area with a distinctive visitor appeal, and whose terrain supports the description of around forty walks of well-varied length and degree of severity, in order to cater for all walking abilities and seasonal conditions.

These format restraints have led to the decision that some of Mary Welsh's earlier Scottish books, written with delight and enthusiasm in the 1990s after visits to the islands like Islay, Coll and Tiree, and the Small Isles needed to be subsumed into longer works covering wider areas, producing full-length volumes of wider appeal and greater commercial viability.

As a first step, Clan books published in 2005 an extended new edition encompassing the isles of Islay, Jura and Colonsay, which formed a geographically logical grouping in the south-west. Here, in this new volume, Mary Welsh and Christine Isherwood have explored the wild and magical lands to the west of Loch Linnhe and the A82 Fort William–Great Glen axis, leading both by geographical logic and historical tradition (hence 'The Road to the Isles' in the title) to the Small Isles of Canna, Rum, Eigg and Muck.

Our sincere wish is that, armed with this book as their guide, readers who love walking will come, and then come again, to discover the joys of the wild mainland and the tantalizing islands that comprise this very special highland wonderland.

In conclusion, we would remind readers that in this series of guides the authors have made every effort to ensure accuracy, but that changes can occur after publication. You should check locally on transport, accommodation, etc. The publisher welcomes any notes of important changes. Neither the publisher nor the authors can accept responsibility for errors, omissions or any loss or injury.

IMPORTANT! Visitors to the Small Isles should note that the ferries carry passengers only. Plan either to reach Mallaig or Arisaig by public transport or to leave your car on the mainland.

Acknowledgements

Our thanks go to both our families, who encouraged us all the way; to Mrs Jenny MacEwen of the Isle of Muck and to Richard Kilpatrick, deputy reserve manager of the Isle of Rum National Nature Reserve, who kindly checked the routes on their respective islands. Our grateful thanks also go to Eilidh-Ann Madden, the forest ranger for Ardnamurchan; to Jake Willis, of the Sunart Oakwoods Initiative, and Isabel Isherwood, for their support, ideas and helpful comments.

Mary Welsh
Christine Isherwood

The Authors' Golden Rules
for Good, Safe Walking

- Wear suitable clothes and take adequate waterproofs.

- Walk in strong footwear; walking boots are advisable.

- Carry the relevant map and know how to use it.

- Take extra food and drink as emergency rations.

- Carry a whistle; remember six long blasts repeated at one minute intervals is the distress signal.

- Do not walk alone, and tell someone where you are going.

- If mist descends, return.

- Keep all dogs under strict control. Observe all 'No Dogs' notices—they are there for very good reasons.

Contents

Contents continued page 6

Drimnin to Doirlinn, Morvern

There is limited parking in Drimnin. The best place is at the pier, grid ref 556539, where there is room for about 3 cars, but park carefully to allow plenty of room for turning. There is also space for a car on the verge by the telephone box, and one or maybe two could be tucked in, with care (not obstructing the gate), at the bottom of the track to Mungosdail, grid ref 561537. To reach the start, take the B849, north from Lochaline to Drimnin, where it ends.

Barr is an old settlement with substantial ruins remaining. The lovely pool below the waterfall is said to be so deep a horse and cart disappeared into it, and were never seen again.

Waterfall at Barr

Loch Teacuis, the outer loch of three, which together almost cut Morvern in half. The loch opens into Loch Sunart but its entrance is nearly blocked by the high rocky island of Carna. The whole loch is fairly inaccessible except on foot; all roads to it are private or unsurfaced. It is rich in wildlife and is the area where Don and Bridget MacAskill carried out their studies of otters.

Oronsay, a tidal island, once supported a large community. The people were cleared to it from a neighbouring estate, Auliston, further along the coast – and then later cleared off it.

1 Walk back from the pier along the road. Cross the burn and go uphill to a track, on the left, with a Scottish Rights of Way sign 'Barr and Kinlochteacuis' (this is the Mungosdail track). Go on uphill through pleasant deciduous woodland, with the burn below to your left. At a junction, take the waymarked right turn by a tributary burn. Above, to your right, are the remains of St. Fintan's Church and a graveyard. Cross the burn on a

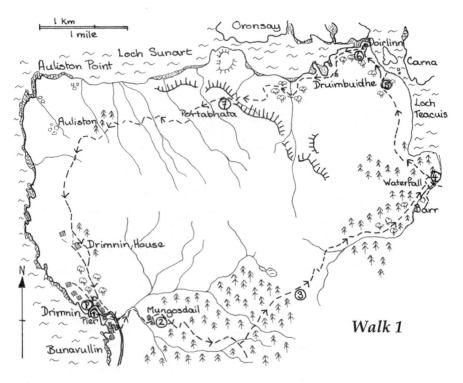

Walk 1

fine stone bridge and continue through a gate and up a left turn to Mungosdail farm. Carry on through the well-kept farm buildings and wind left, then right, along a walled track. Cross a field to a gate into the forest.

Pine Marten

2 Enjoy the track up through the trees. It is delightful, surfaced with moss and quite open. It zigzags up gently, with views, at intervals, across to Mull. Look out for woodcock, especially in winter; and although you may not see pine martens and foxes there are plenty of their droppings along the track. Follow the track for 1 mile/1.5km and then go with it as it curves round to cross a burn by a bridge. A few steps along, take a signed path, climbing steadily, off to the left. Step across two small burns and then continue to a deer gate, with a small wicket gate, out onto the open moor. Go straight ahead up an indistinct path, heading for a waymarked post just below the crest of the ridge. Aim for an obvious notch in the ridge, through which the path continues, and from where you have a fine view across Loch Teacuis to Beinn Iadain and Beinn na h-Uamha.

3 Beyond the ridge the path descends to the left. It is an old postman's path so traces of a very good track remain, and it has been well waymarked. However, if in doubt, look across the valley beyond the burn to the edge of the forest, to see a gate and a ride going into the trees, and aim for this. The going is good on short grass and is reasonably dry (it is basalt country). Beyond the gate the path is flanked by sitka spruce and is somewhat wetter but still good and very obvious. Descend steadily through the dense trees until they begin to open out and birch and rowan appear.

Then an old wall, covered in moss, runs beside the path and soon, the Barr River appears below on the right. Turn left by another old wall and come down to a forest road.

4 If you want to visit the ruined settlement of Barr, turn right here, cross the bridge over the Barr River and turn right again. About 30yds/100m up the track, on the right, is a ruin and behind it the splendid waterfall, with a deep pool, where you may wish to picnic. Then return down the track, re-cross the bridge and carry on the forest track, continuing ahead until you reach its end. There is a sudden magnificent view from here across Loch Teacuis to Carna, the island in the mouth of the loch. A small well-constructed path leaves the end of the track and continues through an area of clearfell, with groups of birch, curving round to form a high terrace above the coast. This clearfell area is being restored to natural oak and birch wood as part of the forestry commission's Sunart Oakwoods initiative. The views are splendid. Below in a large bay you may see heron, wigeon and merganser. Follow the path as it climbs steadily to a low col. Then, where it winds round below a crag, it is unsurfaced for a short distance. Carry on to a gate at the edge of the clearfell and continue. Stop where the path begins to descend steeply towards the shore and the tidal islet beside Eilean nan Eildean, unless you wish to visit the islet.

5 To continue this walk, leave the path at this point and go on, ahead, along the most difficult part of the ramble, for about 650yds/600m. Make your way along the edge of the level ground, through purple moor grass and bog myrtle, heading for a small oakwood. Cross a tiny burn in the wood and climb its far bank to two small ruins perched on the side of a rocky knoll. Pick up a vague path in front of the ruins and contour on it along the knoll then over a dip and steeply down the far side. Cross a bog and go up and round the back of a heather-covered hill, where there is another ruin at the end. Bear left here, slightly uphill, and cross a bracken-covered area to pick up an ancient track. Follow this until you reach the white painted cottage at Doirlinn and a good track.

6 Now begins the most delightful part of this fine walk. Follow the path along the intricate coastline, with the tidal island of Oronsay across the channel, on the right. Head on winding

Reed Bunting

through oak, birch and hazel woodland, round bays and rocky headlands. Look out for otters all along the shore and seals too. In about ½ mile/1km you reach the cottage at Drumbuie. A similar distance, further on, you come to a grassy area by the sea, where the path turns inland. Cross a burn on a stout wooden bridge, where you might spot reed buntings. Cliffs edge the valley and you should look out for golden eagles. Climb steadily on up the path, round a large zigzag (where there is a seat) and then ascend a long traverse below basalt cliffs to the lip of the escarpment. Another seat here is most welcome and faces a spectacular view up Loch Sunart.

7 Stride the path across high moorland, with views over to Ben Hiant on Ardnamurchan. Notice the ruins of various abandoned villages below. There are mileposts by the track so you can see how far you have come and how far you still have to go. Beyond a small plantation, the track starts to zigzag down to reach a burn. (A grassy track on the right going through a gate before the burn leads down to the ruined village of Auliston which you might wish to visit.) The main track goes steadily downhill, rounding a corner below basalt crags, now with the Sound of Mull below and Tobermory coming into view, beyond. Descend through pasture to a deer gate and then down a walled track, with trees to your left. At a junction take the left track, which crosses a gorse-grown pasture and then a small hazel wood. Go through a gate at the far end and go on down a walled track to a gate and stile. Cross and turn left on the access track beyond, which runs through woodland, with primroses in spring. Here

you might spot woodcock. Ignore a track on the left and at the next junction take the right turn downhill, which winds round left, forms the left side of a triangle and then comes down to the road at Drimnin. Turn right to return to the pier.

Primroses, Wood Sorrel and Golden Saxifrage

Practicals

Type of walk: A really long walk, mostly on good paths and tracks, following old postal routes. One short stretch needs careful route finding or navigation skills. Go well prepared (boots, waterproofs etc) as the route takes you through fairly remote country. Stunning views.

Total Distance: 14 miles/23km
Time: 7–8 hours
Maps: OS Explorer 383 / Landranger 47 and 49

Loch Aline and Ardtornish Castle, Morven

Park in a paved parking area, grid ref 679448, beyond the ferry pier for Mull. Do not join the queue for the ferry but bear left along the shore past a rough parking area to reach the paved part. This is reached by taking the A884, the only road into Morvern, and then turning left in the village of Lochaline. Take care not to obstruct access to the mine.

The Sand Mine was developed, during the last war, as a source of silica for making glass for lenses. The sandstone mined is very pure and is amazingly white. The mine is still in production, although today it employs few people compared with over 60 in the 1960s. The output is still high. The workings extend for over 1¼ miles/ 2km into the hill, and over 5 million tons of sand has been removed over the years.

Kinlochaline Castle

Kinlochaline Castle stands above the River Aline where it flows out into the loch.

It is a 15th century tower house which belonged to the MacLeans. It became a ruin but has been restored and is now a private dwelling.

Old Ardtornish Castle was probably built some time in the 13th century and was a stronghold of Clan Donald, Lords of the Isles, until the late 15th century. Later ownership passed to the MacLeans who also owned Duart Castle, opposite, on Mull. Together they controlled the Sound of Mull. In 1701 the MacLeans were succeeded by the Campbells; the castle, soon replaced as a dwelling, fell into disrepair.

1 Walk on along the road towards the mine, round the barrier and then continue on the footpath beside the road. At the mine workings, follow the signs, which direct you round to the right to avoid the working area. Admire the quantities of shining white sand. The path continues beside the track, beyond the workings, until the track turns away up the hill. At this point carry on straight ahead above the shore on the old road, passing through lovely mixed woodland, crossing two fine culverted burns and enjoying good views across the loch. Watch out for curlews and herons, and you may see otters fishing, particularly as you approach the head of the loch. You may also be lucky enough to see a sea eagle.

2 At the head of the loch turn right past a cottage onto a minor road and follow this as it winds left beside the fast-flowing River Aline below

Walk 2

14

Kinlochaline Castle. Cross the bridge over the river and walk on round the bay below the fine gardens of Ardtornish House, which you may like to visit. (To do this, keep left to the estate offices after crossing another bridge. This is also an alternative parking place if you wish to split the walk into two.) The sand flats at the head of the loch are excellent for bird-watching, with wigeon and goldeneye in winter, and greenshank in spring and autumn.

Sea Eagle

3 If you intend to continue to Old Ardtornish Castle, turn right after crossing the second bridge and take the shore road signed to the net station. This is metalled after about 220yds/200m. Take care because traffic does use it. Beyond the net station the road reverts to a track, continuing just above the shore past a wide sheltered inlet where yachts are moored. Go through a deer gate and round the corner; here you are directly opposite Lochaline village and very near to it; it seems a long walk for not much progress. Walk on past two cottages on the left, and a small jetty on the right, then up a long slope onto a wave-cut platform. Continue past a wood of mature trees leaning away from the prevailing south-westerlies. Carry on to a farm steading in more woodland. Go past the buildings, through a gate, and bear right to go through another gate. Stop on the edge of the path to admire the splendid bay below you. It is deeply cut into the coastline and surrounded by steep wooded slopes with cliffs at the top. Several waterfalls plummet spectacularly over the edges; on a windy day you may see these blowing back upwards so that the cliff edges seem to be smoking.

4 Walk on along the wide path, with a fine estate wall to your right and the drop to your left, masked by beech and larch trees. Go

15

through a small gate and across a boggy area, then up to the old ruined castle. Explore carefully because the walls are not secure. Then return by your outward route.

Greenshank

Practicals

Type of walk: A very easy, mainly level linear walk on old roads and tracks. It is long but it can easily be divided into two, using a second car park at the Ardtornish Estate Offices, grid ref 704473.

Total Distance:	14 miles/23km
Time:	5–7 hours
Maps:	OS Explorer 383 / Landranger 49

Achranich to Loch Tearnait, Morvern

Park in the large car park outside the Ardtornish Estate Office, grid ref 704473. Check at the office that you will not be in the way; they are very helpful. To access the parking area, leave the A884, about 4km north of Lochaline, to take the minor road on the right, signed Ardtornish. Cross two rivers and bear left after the second one to the cluster of buildings on the left, which house the Estate Office.

The area at the head of **Loch Aline** is correctly called Achranich, the name Ardtornish (meaning Thor's high point) applying to the peninsula on the outer loch and the old castle. However in 1860 Octavius Smith who owned the Achranich Estate bought Ardtornish too and transferred the name to the whole of his property in Morvern.

Crannogs, built on artificial platforms of stone and wood, were constructed in lochs and bogs. Usually a wooden causeway linked the crannog to the shore. Some causeways were of built of stones and several of these were deliberately left loose. These created a noise when

Loch Tearnait

walked on, providing a warning of the approach of an enemy, to those inside.

Ardtornish House, an enormous mansion set in beautiful grounds, is situated at Achranich at the head of the loch. The grounds are open to the public for a small fee and are quite wild but lovely, especially when the azaleas are flowering.

1 Go round the far side of the Estate Office and through the gate. Bear right across the lawn on an obvious path and cross the wooden footbridge over the Rannoch River. Turn right and go through a deer gate to follow a track through glorious deciduous woodland, with the river to your right. Look for grey wagtails or a dipper here. At a cross of tracks go straight on uphill to pass a house (Riverside) to your right and then another (Hillside) to your left.

2 Go through a deer gate onto rough fellside with scattered trees of oak and birch sloping steeply down to the river on your right. Ignore a track down to a small turbine house and continue uphill above the wood, now with a deer fence and a large waterpipe to the left. The river flows in a spectacular gorge with waterfalls, best seen in winter when there are no leaves on the trees.

3 Beyond a small hydro scheme, the valley flattens out and the path becomes grassier and skirts the edge of the valley. Notice the fine perched boulder on a hill to the right. The path then climbs over a spur and winds round above a large flat area, Strath Shuardail, where three burns cut complex meanders through the bog. The high hill enclosing the strath on the right is Glais Bheinn, with a flat-topped crag at its left end called the Table of Lorn. Descend a long slope to cross one of the burns on a culvert and then climb again over another spur. Admire the

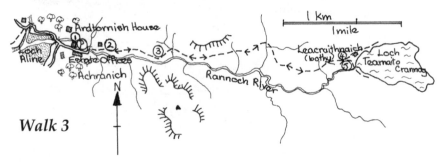

Walk 3

two attractive waterfalls in a narrow gorge. The path now is a pleasant grassy shelf along the hillside. As you come over the ridge, there in front of you is Loch Tearnait, remote and surrounded by hills.

Whooper Swans

4 The island in the loch is a crannog. Look for divers on the loch, and whooper swans in winter, and you may see greenshank in spring and summer. Scan the surrounding skylines for golden and white-tailed eagles; you may even see them interacting if you are very lucky. Where the path divides, take the left branch going a short way uphill to Leacraithnaich bothy, maintained by the Mountain Bothies Association, where you can shelter and eat your lunch if the weather has turned unpleasant. Or take the right branch to go down to the water's edge where the Rannoch River leaves the loch and there is a small dam.

5 When you have finished exploring, retrace your steps down by the Rannoch River to Ardtornish, enjoying the very different views down the glen.

Practicals

Type of walk: A straightforward walk on a track the whole way. It becomes grassy and occasionally wet in its further reaches but remains easy to walk. The views are fine and the loch remote and beautiful.

Total Distance: 5 miles/8km
Time: 3 hours
Maps: OS Explorer 383 / Landranger 49

Ardtornish Estate stalk deer from mid-August to mid-October but there is usually no problem with this walk. However you should check at the office in the stalking season.

4

Beinn Iadain from Kinlochteacuis, Morvern

Park in a space, grid ref 656541, at the end of the public road, where there is room for two or three cars, if parked carefully. This is accessed by the minor road to Rahoy, which leaves the A884 after 3 miles/5 km north of Lochaline.

Beinn Iadain, one of the highest hills in Morvern is 1880ft/ 571m in height. It has an enjoyable narrow ridge leading up to its summit. Both it, and its neighbour Beinn na-h-Uamha, are capped with layers of basalt which forms open gravelly areas on the summits, and these are noted for their interesting flora. **The Rahoy Hills Wildlife Reserve** was set up largely to protect these special areas for conservation. As you climb you are asked only to look at the plants, not to pick, and to avoid trampling on them by keeping to the paths, where possible.

Beinn Iadain

Walk 4

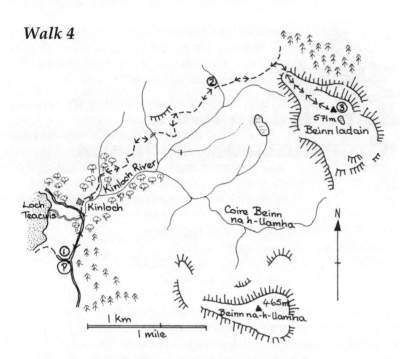

1 From where you have parked, walk on along the private road towards Rahoy. Go through the gate and on to cross the burn. At the junction, just beyond, take the reinforced track, right, signed to Kinloch. Go uphill and pass to the right of the farm buildings. Keep straight ahead. Ignore the track on the right, which goes to Kinloch House. Go through the pedestrian gate to the left of a deer gate and continue through scattered woodland of oak, birch and alder. Wind left, and then right, past a sheep dip enclosure on the right and more woodland on the left. Then leave the trees behind and follow the good track up the side of a wide valley with fine views of Beinn Iadain ahead and Beinn na h-Uamha to the right. Look for snipe, feeding in the wetter areas by the track, and in spring and early summer listen for their drumming. You

Snipe

might also spot curlew. The path climbs steadily, makes a big zigzag up the valley side and then contours. Red deer frequent the hillside in some numbers.

Purple Saxifrage

2 At a small quarry the old path becomes a more recent track, not shown on the map. It takes you on up the valley, along the edge of a small ravine, onto the shoulder of the hill below Beinn Iadain. Here, at the right time of the year, you might see snow buntings and, in summer, look for golden plovers. When you reach another small quarry in a knoll, leave the track and wind round the side of the knoll using traces of a path to come to a high stile over a deer fence. Cross and make your way to the ridge leading to the summit of Beinn Iadain. Climb the indistinct path up the fine steep-sided narrow ridge and follow it as it winds in and out of the rocky outcrops, or do some easy scrambling if you prefer. Look for purple saxifrage in spring and mossy saxifrage in early summer. At the top, climb the fence and walk up to the trig point. Continue on along the top to come to a delightful small lochan, partly visible from the trig point and cradled between low crags.

3 Return by the route of ascent.

Mossy Saxifrage

Practicals

Type of walk: Linear. Very straightforward ascent by the track to the shoulder. The ridge is quite exposed and although not difficult in good conditions, it should not be attempted in high winds, and it is impossible in snow without crampons.

Total Distance:	7½ miles/12km
Time:	4–5 hours
Maps:	OS Explorer 383 / Landranger 49

5

The ruined township of Inniemore (Aoineadh Mor), Morvern

Park in the forestry commission car park, signed 'Aoineadh Mor', grid ref 668527. This lies 2½ miles/4 km along the minor road to Rahoy and Kinlochteacuis, which leaves the A 884 about 3 miles/5 km north of Lochaline.

In 1824 the land, including **Inniemore**, was sold by the Duke of Argyll, to Miss Christina Stewart who lived in Edinburgh. She knew nothing of the land and was advised that the best way to make it pay would be to evict the people and bring in sheep. The people offered to pay higher rents but their request was

Aoineadh Mor (Inniemore) deserted village

turned down. All were driven out of their homes and the houses demolished. They were not allowed to reap their crops or milk their goats. Mary and James Cameron were among those evicted; Mary carried the baby and looked after the two older children whilst James carried his old mother on his back. Later, in Glasgow, Mary recounted their experiences to the son of the minister who recorded them.

The Forestry Commission bought and planted the land in 1930, using the labour of the people evacuated from St. Kilda. No notice was taken of the old houses, indeed many trees were actually planted inside them. When the area was felled, in 1990, **the village was rediscovered**. The felling was therefore done with great care, and the new paths put in.

1 Take the left path of two, which lead out of the car park. It goes round by picnic tables, then winds right and climbs steeply to contour round the hillside. On the right is deciduous woodland, full of bluebells in spring; and on the left, spruce, with goldcrests and coal tits. Once over an open area the path descends briefly to join another. Turn left, then at a Y-junction 110yds/100m further on, take the right branch named Mary's path. This is a delightful section of the walk, running along the hillside through oak and birch. Gradually the path descends to continue beside a wall; the trees are now all spruce but the views across the wall are open. Pine martens use this path regularly and you will find their droppings at intervals.

2 After a short uphill stretch, take a path on the right, which leads through a wall gap into open (felled) ground, the low land of a hidden valley cradled below the dramatic basalt escarpment of Aoineadh Mor (from which the township took its name). Go along the path to a board, which shows the layout of the old township. Then return 22yds/20m along the path and take another path, now on your left, which winds down among the old ruined houses and kailyards (vegetable

Walk 5

24

patches). Cross the bridge over the burn and turn left. The paths on this side are no longer maintained but are still visible at the time of writing. After a boggy stretch beside the burn, turn uphill past a substantial ruin, then go right to the next ruin, and on uphill round an old kailyard. The path winds on across the hillside and from its highest point there is an excellent view over the whole settlement. Imagine how it must all have looked when fifteen families lived and worked here. Now it is populated only by tree pipits and stonechats.

Tree Pipit

3 Descend a steep grassy slope and return to the bank of the burn. Turn right, to come to the bridge. Cross again and turn right to wind through the ruins on this side of the valley up to the old wall or 'head dyke' which surrounded the township, and then come back, finally, to the information board at the top. Return to the wall gap and path junction where you entered the cleared area.

4 Take the path called James' path, which goes uphill away from the village. It winds up through spruce, then runs along the hill, high up, from where there are fine views over to Loch Doire nam Mart and, ahead, to Beinn na h-Uamha. Then you come steeply down steps to join Mary's path, and walk ahead to the next path junction. Take the left branch, which goes downhill through lovely woodland and along the valley floor back to the car park.

Practicals

Type of walk: This is a pleasant walk along well-made paths, steep in places, to an interesting ruined township. Some of the paths round the township, beyond the burn, are boggy and indistinct but are worth exploring.

Total Distance: 2 miles/3.4km
Time: 2 hours
Maps: OS Explorer 383 / Landranger 49

6

Loch Arienas Point, Morvern

Park in the small car park, grid ref 702503, at the entrance to the Scottish Wildlife Trust, Rahoy Hills Reserve, at Acharn Bridge. This is reached by the A844, north west of Lochaline.

Acharn and Arienas were both cleared villages like Inniemore,walk 5. Spend some time looking at the ruined houses. The lade bringing water from the Abhainn Dubh to the corn mills in Acharn is still very clear.

Some **chambered cairns** were possibly used first in the second or third millenium BC and later in the early Bronze Age. The chambers were concealed by an enormous cairn of stone. It is believed that they were used as a collective burial site for the local inhabitants of the area and possibly for rituals.

Loch Arienas

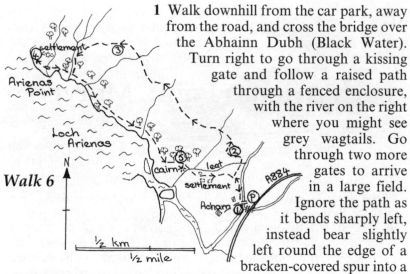

Walk 6

N

½ km

½ mile

1 Walk downhill from the car park, away from the road, and cross the bridge over the Abhainn Dubh (Black Water). Turn right to go through a kissing gate and follow a raised path through a fenced enclosure, with the river on the right where you might see grey wagtails. Go through two more gates to arrive in a large field. Ignore the path as it bends sharply left, instead bear slightly left round the edge of a bracken-covered spur into a hollow with an old mill lade. This carried water from the Abhainn Dubh down to the old settlement of Acharn. Cross the lade on stones and head up the hillside opposite, making for a fine oak tree halfway up. Join an old path, which climbs across the hillside, crosses a burn and then winds round a rocky knoll to go through a gate.

2 Climb directly up the steep hill to a shoulder where a path, well used by animals, turns left and begins to contour. Cross a burn on stones and head for a small col where a deer fence appears on your left. Walk on the level way above the fence. Enjoy the splendid views out over Loch Arienas to the basalt escarpment beyond and, behind, down towards Loch Aline and Mull. Look for snipe in the marshy places and stonechats perching on the fence and chacking. After about ½ mile/1 km the fence turns away downhill but this walk continues to contour on the small path. Loch Arienas and the Point is now below and slightly ahead.

3 Follow the path as it makes a sharp turn downhill and becomes more distinct. Descend into oak woodland and bear left down the left bank of a burn. Turn right onto a wide distinct path. Cross the burn on well-laid stepping stones and walk on through bracken and scattered iris to a footbridge over the next burn. The delightful open area ahead, surrounded by fine mature trees, is Arienas Point. The ruins of the old village of Arienas can be seen

Black-throated Diver

uphill to the right. Spend some time exploring and enjoying the views. Black-throated divers, cormorants and whooper swans use the loch in their appropriate seasons, and if you are very lucky you could see a sea eagle fly over.

4 Return over the bridge and then the stepping stones. Follow the lovely well-kept path above the shore. Beyond another burn go through a sloping deer gate at the edge of an oak wood. Carry on along the distinct path as it goes up and down through small woods and some bogs. Finally descend steeply through more trees to go through another deer gate. Keep left beside the fence, with a pool on the right, beyond which the river leaves Loch Arienas in a fine series of sand-bars. Walk on by the fence, round a corner and uphill.

5 Opposite a gate in the fence look right to see a large chambered cairn, mostly ruinous but with two chambers still visible. Cross a stile in the fence beyond, then follow the clear waymarked path through the old village of Acharn (to which the mill lade flowed) and along above the remains of the lade. Go past two large ash trees to rejoin your outward path. Turn right through the gate and go along the raised way to the bridge. Cross and return to your car. From here look at the fine old road bridge down on the right.

Practicals

Type of walk: A lovely walk with fine views and lots of historic interest. The upper path is used by animals so is muddy and not always clear but it is worth looking for; the lower (return) path has been put in by the Scottish Wildlife Trust and is very good.

Total Distance: 2 miles/3.5km
Time: 2 hours
Maps: OS Explorer 383 / Landranger 49

7

The Black Glen (Gleann Dubh), Morvern

Park in the small car park, grid ref, 702503, for the Rahoy Hills Nature Reserve (owned by Ardtornish Estate and managed by the Scottish Wildlife Trust) 3¾ miles/6km north of Lochaline. The car park is on the west side of the road by the bridge at Acharn. To reach this, take the A884 to Lochaline.

Crosben was designed and built by Samuel Barham.as a shepherd's cottage in 1881–2. Barham, an Englishman, was employed on the Ardtornish Estate from 1870 as 'Master of Works'. The first building for which his plans survive was the Achranich coach house built in 1871–2, and this and all his later buildings were built of concrete. The designs are characteristic, with high gables, enormous eaves and decorated barge boards.

Crosben

Golden Eagle

The **track from Acharn to Crosben** was built as an estate road in 1872–3. This and the track to Loch Tearnait, built at the same time, cost £1,500, a considerable sum in those days.

1 Look at the new interpretive boards in the car park and then walk up the good track past a noticeboard and on into oak wood-land. Listen for wood warblers and tree pipits as you go. The river, the Black Water or Abhainn Dubh, is visible on the left at the start but soon vanishes into a gorge, and the bank to your left slopes off very steeply. Continue up the track, which rises gently to cross open ground with a fence on the right. It then moves back into the trees and runs along the top of the wood. In spring the wood is a sea of bluebells and the trees are the haunt of song birds. The track goes through a gate gap, then dips to cross two small burns, with primroses on their banks. As you go higher up the glen the river gorge is less deep and you can catch glimpses of the water through the trees. Go down onto a boggy promontory to view a series of three small but attractive water-falls, which are dramatic when the river is in spate. Then return to the track and carry on into more open birch woodland. Admire the spec-tacular boulders scattered about the hillside, some of which look like ancient standing stones, although in fact they are all natural.

Walk 7

30

Look along the skyline where you might spot a soaring golden eagle. At the right time of the year, listen for the many cuckoos.

2 Cross the Black Water on a good bridge, from where you might see grey wagtails and common sandpipers by the water's edge. Walk on into a wide remote glen watching for deer on the flats, or on the skyline in summer, when they try to avoid the midges. Pass the ruin of a quite substantial crofthouse. The dramatic hill, which appears in the gap at the head of the glen, is Garbh Bheinn (of Ardgour). Continue gently downhill on the good track into a side valley and cross it towards another house, not ruined this time, standing at the foot of a tree-lined gorge. This is Crosben, designed by Samuel Barham.

3 On reaching a rather ricketty bridge, the track ends. Retrace your steps back down the glen, enjoying the fine views across to Dun na Gaoithe on Mull between the trees.

Grey Wagtails

Practicals

Type of walk: This is a lovely easy linear walk up a delightful glen, wooded at first and then wide and open. The track is good all the way.

Total Distance: 6–7miles/9.5–11.4km
Time: 3–4 hours
Maps: OS Explorer 383 / Landranger 49

8

Ardgour and Clovullin

Park on the shore side of the A861, overlooking Loch Linnhe, grid ref 016637, just beyond the 19th century Ardgour Inn. To reach this drive south from Fort William on the A82, towards Onich, and cross the Corran Narrows on the inexpensive ferry (5 minutes) to the peninsula side of Loch Linnhe. Or you may prefer to use the car park on the Onich side and then take the ferry to Corran, free to pedestrians.

Thomas Telford, besides designing canals, bridges and the Corran slipway, oversaw the construction of more than 30 churches. These included **Ardgour church**, which was built in 1832. It was the only one to have a vestry. Here the minister would change his wet clothes after being rowed across the loch from his home on the opposite side of Loch Linnhe.

Corran Narrows is one of the oldest trade routes in the Highlands, the original road to the isles. Then the ferry was just a

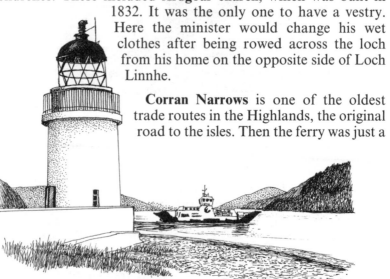

Corran

rowing boat and cattle drovers would have swum their cattle across the narrows. The first car ferry came into service in 1935 and took only two cars. Today, though there are two ferries, only one is in service at any time, a little one in winter and a

Black Guillemot

larger one in summer. Between them they carry a quarter of a million cars each year. At the end of the pier that stands a little north of the jetty, several bird boxes have been fixed to the upper rail. These provide nest sites for black guillemots which make full use of them.

In summer time you have just a glimpse of the two **kettle hole lochs** through the dense foliage of the trees. Kettle holes are bowl-shaped hollows in the moraine (loose rocks and gravel) that has been left behind by a melting glacier. Large pieces of ice become separated from the main body of the glacier. These leave holes where they have rested. Many kettle holes are filled with water and form lochs, others exist as small swamps.

1 From the parking area, walk on past the pier, enjoying the view up the lovely loch, where tier after tier of mountain slopes descend steeply to the water's edge. After passing the dwellings of North Corran, cross the road to visit the pretty parish church of Ardgour.

2 Turn left immediately beyond the church to walk a track towards Ardgour House. Pass through a small gate, beside a large locked one, and go on along the level way through deciduous woodland. Here flourish rhododendrons and foxgloves, colourful in

Walk 8

33

early summer. As you continue look through the lofty trees, on the left, to see the first kettlehole loch. Ignore the next left turn and carry on past a larger loch.

3 At the metalled road, turn left and walk on to pass through large ornate gates onto the road at Clovullin. On the other side of the road, behind a hedge, is a shop, tearoom and petrol station, with its own parking area.

4 Bear left and walk the quiet way to join the A861. Turn left again and walk along the verge on the left side. When level with a bungalow, cross, and where the Japanese knotweed ends, descend a little path onto the beach. Continue along the shore and wind round the outside of the ornate lighthouse and then join the road again where the cars queue for the ferry. If the tide is too high then remain on the A-road.

Foxglove

Practicals

Type of walk: Pleasing short stroll beside Loch Linnhe and then on level estate tracks. The return is made along the grass verges of two roads and then over a shingle beach.

Total Distance: 1½ miles/2.5km
Time: 1 hour
Maps: OS Explorer 391 / Landranger 41

9

Ariundle and Fee Donald Mine, Ardnamurchan

Park in the forestry car park, grid ref 826633, at the end of the road. To reach this, cross the bridge in Strontian village and turn right off the A861 to drive up the minor road, west of the burn, signed to Ariundle. After a mile take the right branch at a Y-junction and carry on to the end of the surfaced road.

Strontian River and Sgurr Dhomhnuill

Ariundle Oakwood is a National Nature Reserve. It is a remnant of the oakwood that used to cover all the low ground in the wet sheltered valleys of the western seaboard. The oaks are sessile and have been growing here since they colonised the area at the end of the last Ice Age. They were harvested by coppicing in the late 18th and early 19th centuries to supply charcoal to the iron furnace at Bonawe on Loch Etive. When this closed the market for the wood disappeared and animals were allowed to graze the woods, preventing regeneration. Now that sheep are excluded and deer managed, the woods are returning to their former glory.

Lead has been mined in the valleys behind Strontian village since at least 1722 (first record). There were five mines, of which Fee Donald (wrongly named Bellsgrove on the OS map), the most easterly and Corrantee, the most westerly, are only accessible on foot. The other three, Bellsgrove, Middleshop and Whitesmith are near the road from Strontian to Polloch on Loch Shiel. The mines closed down towards the end of the 19th century, following a crash in the world prices for lead. The mineral **strontianite**, containing the element strontium, was first discovered associated with the lead in these mines, mainly in the central group, although it is not common even there.

1 Return to the track from the car park and turn right up the glen. There are wide open views, because many of the conifers have been removed to return the woodland to its original state. Then the trees close in, with Scots pine on the right and mixed oak and birch uphill on the left. Take the second waymarked path on the right to wind down through the trees and cross the Strontian River on a sturdy bridge. Turn left to follow the riverbank up the glen.

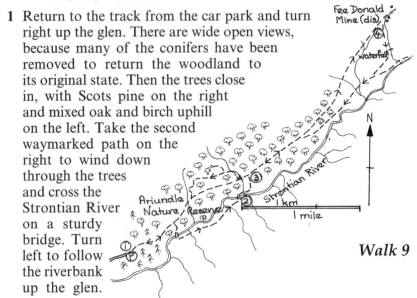

Walk 9

Enjoy the magnificent views up the glen to Sgurr Dhomhnuill and Sgurr na h-Ighinn. The river is lined with gorse, which in spring glows golden and gives off a strong scent of coconut in the sunshine. Wood anemones flower in the grass, and dippers may be seen on the rocks in the water. Up the hillside on the right you can see the ridge and furrow marks of old run-rig cultivation, now dotted with young trees.

Chequered Skipper

2 Cross the river again at the next bridge and continue walking upstream on the far bank to a fence with a kissing gate, the entrance to the National Nature Reserve. Go through into open woodland and bear left along the path, with a boardwalk over boggy areas. The way becomes drier as it gets higher into oak and birch wood.

3 At the track junction turn right onto the old way up the valley to the mine, a delightful well-made track, which rises gently across the hillside, through woodland for much of the way. Soon there is a deer-fenced 'exclosure' on the left. Notice how much bilberry grows inside compared with the grazed slopes outside, and how many more saplings grow inside the fence. Go through the kissing gate beside a deer gate marking the end of the Nature Reserve. Go on to take the left branch at the Y-junction, which continues uphill with a fence on the left and a steep slope on the right. Follow the path as it runs along a pleasing mossy terrace, with glimpses of the mountains through the trees. Beyond the next deer gate, the path crosses a burn in a deep gully on what appears to be a rather ricketty bridge. In fact the bridge seems perfectly firm, at the time of writing, but you cross it at your own risk. If you do not want to try you should return from here. Emerge onto the open hillside, with striking views up the glen where Sgurr na h-Ighinn is the dominant hill, with Sgurr Dhomhnuill peeping over its shoulder and Sgurr a'Chaorainn to the right. Follow the continuing track as it curves round the hillside, left, high above the glen of the Strontian river, into the side valley of the Allt Feith Dhomhnuill, the burn which gave its name to the old lead mine. The spoil heaps and remains of old mine buildings come into view as you climb and are soon reached. Spend some time exploring and looking for bits of galena (lead ore) on the heaps, but do not attempt to enter the old tunnels, which are dangerous.

4 When you have finished pottering at the mine, turn right beside the burn (do not cross) and pick up a small path which climbs steeply down beside waterfalls into the valley below. Bear right above scattered trees lower down and follow the somewhat wet path along the valley floor, fording three burns. Join the end of a track beside some old buildings and walk up it to rejoin your outward track at the Y-junction just outside the Nature Reserve. Turn left along the track until you reach the place where you emerged onto it from the nature trail. Carry straight on here to cross a burn on a stout bridge, then, almost immediately, turn right onto the Woodland Walk, a winding path which goes uphill following the bank of the burn and then turning away and levelling out. Take a path branching off to the right which leads uphill to a large mound, believed to be the site of an Iron Age round house. Then return to the main path and turn right to continue through the woodland. Head up the path, over duck boarding on wet areas, cross a burn, then climb steeply into a pleasant high pasture with a ruined croft. You might spot slow-worms basking here on sunny days. Cross the edge of the open area and drop back down into the woods, watching out for roe deer among the trees. The path zigzags downhill and finally rejoins the track, where you turn right to walk back to the car park.

Practicals

Type of walk: A delightful walk on surfaced paths, boardwalks and an old track.

Total Distance:	7 miles/11.4km
Time:	3–4 hours
Maps:	OS Explorer 391 / Landranger 40

Late news
The forestry commission has just put in a new path linking Strontian village with the above walk. If you wish to extend the walk, park in Strontian in the large car park by the tourist information office and follow signs for the 'Community Woodland'. The new path, signed from here, joins the above walk at the first bridge over the Strontian River – adding 2 miles to the walk.

Beinn Resipol,
Ardnamurchan

There is space for a few cars by the shore just beyond the bridge over the Resipole Burn, grid ref 721639, opposite the track to the Resipole Gallery. Please do not park in the caravan site. The parking area lies on the A861, 6 miles west of Strontian

Beinn Resipol is a Corbett, at 2746ft/845m. It is not all that much lower than a Munro. From Loch Sunart it looks a deceptively wide and rounded hill but its summit ridge is narrow and rocky. Because of its iso-lated position it com-mands one of the finest views along the west Highland coast, including the whole Ardnamurchan penin-sula and mountains from Ben More on Mull to Ben Nevis and its surrounding hills and on round to the Cuillin on Skye.

CMIsherwood *Beinn Resipol*

Walk 10

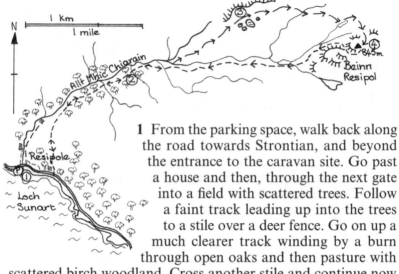

1 From the parking space, walk back along the road towards Strontian, and beyond the entrance to the caravan site. Go past a house and then, through the next gate into a field with scattered trees. Follow a faint track leading up into the trees to a stile over a deer fence. Go on up a much clearer track winding by a burn through open oaks and then pasture with scattered birch woodland. Cross another stile and continue now with the main burn, the Allt Mhic Chiarain, to your left. Gradually the track becomes a footpath, which, though distinct, can be muddy after rain, so you may have to pick your way. At a cairn, cross a tributary burn on stones and bear right along a ridge, then across a bog to a gate. Here you may prefer to stride over the fence in wet weather to avoid the worst part of the bog near the gate. In spring willow warblers sing in the birches and cuckoos call.

Golden Plover

2 The path comes close to the edge of the Allt Mhic Chiarain gorge. Choose any of the several paths as they join up again later. The summit of Beinn Resipol is now in view, looking narrow and elegant and a long way off. Eventually come down a rather awkward wet slope to a junction between a tributary burn and the Allt Mhic Chiarain. The main path crosses the tributary on stones and continues up the right hand side of the Allt Mhic Chiarain, but for a variation on this, and some drier walking, cross the main burn and pick up a sheep track climbing the bank beyond to a terrace. When this runs out, climb steeply up a grassy slope to the next level area. Listen, in spring, for the melancholy piping of golden plovers, and look for them standing on tussocks. You may also see dotterel higher up. Look ahead to see a ridge with a broad grassy swathe up it and make for this, climbing the steep swathe to the top. From here the view up Loch Shiel is stunning and the walking along the top of the ridge is relatively easy.

3 Go round the end of three small lochans, on the northern (Loch Shiel) side of the ridge, and then cross a dip. Beyond it, climb a grassy slope, trending right to walk along a ridge with rocky outcrops. Then bear right across a wide bowl to a burn and follow it up towards the skyline. Go on over fairly level ground and then cross another burn, on stones or a step, to reach the north side of the summit cone of Beinn Resipol. This is well protected with cliffs and if you like scrambling you can find plenty; however there are grassy rakes between the crags, which give steep but quite easy access to the summit ridge. There is a final short rocky pull up to the top, which is small, neat and crowned with a fine two-storey cairn. Enjoy the superb view.

4 When you are ready to descend look for a path continuing down the hill in a south-westerly direction. It goes down quite steeply to a grassy area with a huge rock ahead. Wind round to the right, before the rock, and follow faint paths down between the crags; they look steep but are quite straightforward. Come down to the side of a burn, the Allt Mhic Chiarain again, and turn left on a clear path to follow the burn downhill. It is wet in places and you may like to indulge in burn-hopping to take advantage of the drier ground on the far side. Cross back again before the burn goes over a waterfall into a narrow gorge and stay with the main path along the steep side of the gorge until it opens out. Descend gently to the place where you crossed the burn on your way up and retrace your steps to Resipole.

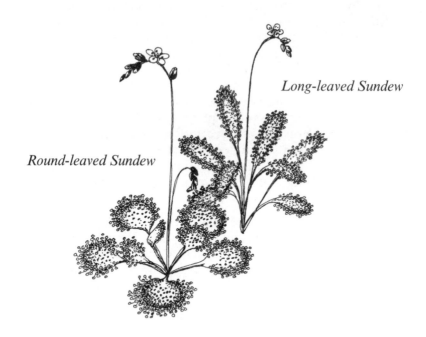

Long-leaved Sundew

Round-leaved Sundew

Practicals

Type of walk: This is a fine climb but definitely not an easy option. It is a strenuous walk starting at sea level. The north ridge, up which this walk goes, is diffuse and should not be attempted in mist unless you are very competent in the use of map and compass; but it would be a shame to do this climb in mist and miss the superb views.

Total Distance: About 7 miles/11.4km
Time: 6–7 hours
Maps: OS Explorer 390 / Landranger 40

Sunart Oakwoods, Ardnamurchan

The woods are among the last remnants of the temperate rainforest oakwoods which once fringed the Atlantic Coast of Britain, and which have been there since the ice retreated after the last glaciation. They are home to many uncommon species, particularly mosses and liverworts. In the past they were used for their timber and many areas were felled and replaced with non-native conifers. Now they are being restored.

Garbh Eilean Hide

Walk 11a Garbh Eilean Hide, Ard Airigh (Ardery)

Park in the Forestry Commission car park, grid ref 746619, signed Ard Airigh. This lies 5miles/8km west of Strontian.

The hide has recently been opened. It is built of local oak, with a turf roof and is fully accessible to those of limited mobility for whom the special car park has been built.

1 Walk out of the car park to the right, and curve round a rocky outcrop. Take the right turn at a junction to cross a flat area and then climb up through larch trees. The path, well made and surfaced with wood chippings, descends steps and then climbs again to cross a knoll with oak woodland down to the left and fine views across to Beinn Resipol on the right. Go down more steps and turn left on the path at the bottom. This brings you down to the hide overlooking Garbh Eilean on Loch Sunart. Spend some time here. Seals, and frequently otters, are seen from this hide. There is a heronry on one of the islands and you might see sea eagles.

2 When you have watched all you want at Garbh Eilean, retrace your steps to the path junction near the car park. Take the right turn here and wind round and up onto a low hill with a seat, from where there is a splendid view down Loch Sunart. Then go back a few yards and follow the path through a shallow cleft in the rocks and down through woodland towards an inlet. Curve round left back to the car park.

Practicals

Type of walk: A pleasant easy walk on good paths to an excellent hide and to a viewpoint

Total Distance: 1½ miles/2.5km
Time: 1 hour
Maps: OS Explorer 390 / Landranger 40

The Nature of Ardnamurchan

NADURRA VISITOR CENTRE
GLENMORE ACHARACLE
TEL: 01972 500209
VAT NO. 991 7268 73

MC #01

REG May   19-08-2014 14:56   016199
May

1	WALKING GLENFINN	£6.99
	1 No	

AMOUNT DUE	**£6.99**
CASH	£10.00
CHANGE GIVEN	£3.01

ZERO SALES	£6.99
ZERO AMOUNT	£0.00

MORAN TAING!
THANK YOU FOR CALLING
PLEASE CALL AGAIN

Salen Oakwoods

Inn
Salen

Park in the car park on the left of the A861 at Salen, grid ref 699645, just before the left turn onto the B8007.

1 Go through the gate at the opposite (south) end of the car park from the village. Follow the delightful path as it winds down through the oak and hazel below the road. In spring this wood is carpeted with primroses. Go through a tall gate and turn left to climb steps to a higher level. Curve left up a valley and then along the rocky side of the hill, then descend gently to a waymarked post at the farthest point of the walk. Carry on round to the right, with tantalising glimpses of the loch below. The slopes are steep but the path is good. After a while it runs in a series of shallow valleys on the side of the headland, before coming back down to the gate again. Walk the remaining short distance to the car park.

An Cnap

A861

Loch
Sunart

¼ Km

¼ mile

Walk 11b

Practicals

Type of walk: A lovely short walk on a good clear path. It is particularly fine in spring when the primroses are out.

Total Distance:	About 1 mile/1.5km
Time:	1 hour
Maps:	OS Explorer 390 / Landranger 40

11c

Glen Borrodale
RSPB Reserve

Park in the small car park, grid ref 601608, provided by the
RSPB. It lies on the right of the road just beyond Glenborrodale
House. To reach this turn left at Salen onto the B8007 and carry
on for a further 8 miles.

1 Turn right out of the car park and take a waymarked path on the
right leading up into the woodland. This is a pleasing path
through woods full of primroses and wood anemones in spring,
and loud with birdsong. Look for redstarts, wood and willow
warblers, and tree creepers. The path climbs steadily up the side
of a valley, then emerges from the trees onto open ground at the

Redstart

Walk 11c

top. There is a lot of wet ground covered in bog myrtle and purple moor grass, but the path stays close to the steeper valley side and avoids most of this. Come down to cross a turbulent burn on a bridge, then at a path junction take the way-marked path which goes down to the left. This path descends through deciduous woodland to join the road. Turn left and walk back carefully (although the road is not busy) to your car. Enjoy the open views across Loch Sunart, and the complex indented coastline, and look out for seals and otters.

Bog Myrtle

Practicals

Type of walk: Another lovely woodland walk, though with more open ground. The path is clear and well waymarked.

Total Distance: About 2 miles/3.4km
Time: 1½ hours
Maps: OS Explorer 390 / Landranger 40 and 47

12

Ben Hiant and Camas nan Geall, Ardnamurchan

Park in the car park for Camas nan Geall, grid 562616. Alternative car park, if climbing only Ben Hiant, is in the small quarry at the top of the hill, grid ref 551641. Access to both parking areas is by the B8007 from Salen to Kilchoan and Ardnamurchan Point.

Cross Stone, Camas nan Geall

This **fine climb** can be divided up in several ways. It can be made into two short walks, one to Camus nan Geall from the car park and the other from the small quarry at the top of the road along the ridge to the summit of Ben Hiant. In both cases, a round walk can be made, by heading for the ruined village of Bourblaige and following the fence, above it, to a track leading out to the road.

Ben Hiant (1659ft/528m), a fine hill out towards the end of the Ardnamurchan penninsula, is volcanic in origin. It is part of the great complex which makes up the peninsula though younger (about 60 million years old) than the volcanic ring out at the end, see walk 13. Because of its situation, it commands splendid

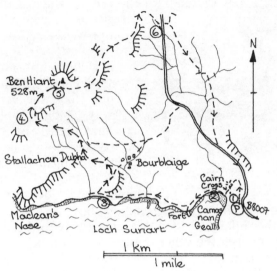

views out to Rum, Eigg and Muck to the north, with Mull to the south.

Camus nan Geall has a fine assemblage of archaeological remains. Look for a Neolithic chambered cairn (4000 BC); a Bronze Age standing stone (2000 BC) with, later, a cross incised into its seaward face, and an aisled cemetery (18th century). There is also an Iron Age fort (600 BC) on the promontory above Sgeir Fhada.

1 Walk down the track from the car park, which leads towards the beach. Go through the kissing gate in the deer fence at the bottom and turn left to the beach. At the end of a row of sycamores, go through a gate gap on the right and look for the ruined chambered cairn; only the large stone slabs remain. Return to the path and go on towards the beach. There is a small iron gate on the left which leads to the aisled graveyard, but in summer this is very much overgrown with bracken. Go round the outside of the cemetery and look for the standing stone. Then continue towards the beach, going through another kissing gate in the deer fence. Turn right and walk above the shore.

2 Cross a burn, which could be difficult in spate; if this is so you will have to return after an enjoyable short stroll. Carry on along

49

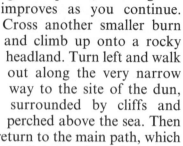

Grass of Parnassus

the back of the beach, which is quite rocky and rough in places, although it improves as you continue. Cross another smaller burn and climb up onto a rocky headland. Turn left and walk out along the very narrow way to the site of the dun, surrounded by cliffs and perched above the sea. Then return to the main path, which soon divides, the left branch going steeply down to the shore through a cleft, the right carrying on above the cliffs to round a gully further inland. It then descends gently to the shore again and joins up with the other branch. Walk on behind the shore over flower-rich turf. Herons fish from rocks and red-throated divers call from out on the water. Ringed plovers and oyster-catchers frequent the pebble beaches, and if you are very lucky you may see an otter.

3 Climb the path to cross the next headland, where a fine basalt dyke comes down to the shore. Carry on round behind the shore until you reach a fence. Do not cross but turn right and climb the hillside up beside it. Less than ¼ mile/0.5km. up, you can see the ruined village of Bourblaige, hidden in its valley. (If you wish to explore the old settlement, continue on up). To carry on with the walk, go through a gate, on the left, before you reach the village. Climb a distinct animal track onto a ridge and turn right to follow it upward. Cross an old wall and go up, left, onto a narrow rocky ridge. Head on up, first on one side of the ridge and then the other, until you find a very well-defined animal path crossing in front of you. Here, turn right and follow this round towards the lip of an inner corrie. Cross the corrie, which is boggy, and walk round above the bog on the north side, joining a distinct path. The path finally peters out below a low col on the ridge of Ben Hiant. Climb the steep grassy slopes to the col and admire the fine view across to Kilchoan. You may see deer.

4 Turn right and zigzag up the steep slope in front, avoiding the rocky outcrops. Follow a broad grassy swathe, beside a bog, up into a basin, where you should climb the drier slopes to its left

50

and walk along the ridge. Wind round and over more knolls until you meet the main path and continue on it to the summit. This is small and rocky, with a cylindrical trig point and a fine cairn. The view is spectacular.

5 Descend by the main path from the summit and wind round left to traverse a steep grassy slope. Admire the cliffs surrounding the top. Descend the path, which is sometimes steep and sometimes level, and go on down the ridge. The views are superb, and the whole ridge walk is a delight. Towards the end you can see the road below; the path bears right, crosses a bog and then a small burn. Continue down beside the burn to the road.

6 Turn left and walk uphill to take a track, on the right, to a small quarry (the alternative parking place). Here look for an indistinct path (the old road) on the right in the edge of the bracken uphill from the telegraph poles. The first part of the way is very hard to follow in high summer because of the ubiquitous plant. Gradually the level way becomes more distinct. Then an old wall appears on the right. Where a burn cuts across the track, go through the wall and descend a little, then zigzag left and cross the burn. Carry on down and then round to cross a wider burn below a fine waterfall. From now on the path becomes gradually clearer. Cross another burn above a waterfall. Follow the path as it climbs a little before it begins to descend the obvious way to the road. Continue along the road to the car park.

Practicals

Type of walk: Exhilarating walking whether you manage the whole circuit or the shorter round.

Total Distances: Complete round 7 miles/11.4km
Shorter round 4 miles/6.6km
Time: 4–5 hours. 3–4 hours
Maps: OS Explorer 390 / Landranger 47

13

Glendrian and the Ardnamurchan Ring

Park in the small quarry about ½ mile/1km before Achnaha, grid ref 469678. If using two cars, leave the other in the good car park at Sanna, grid ref 448693. To reach this drive north from Kilchoan and take the right turn at a Y junction, signed to Sanna and Achnaha.

Before starting this walk you might like to visit the **Natural History Centre at Glen Borrodale**, where there are excellent displays covering the geology and the formation of the Ardnamurchan Ring. There is also a very good café there.

The **Ardnamurchan Ring** is a huge volcanic complex formed when the Atlantic Ocean was opening up. The enormous ring dyke seen today is the remains of probably two volcanoes. They are weathered down to their 'roots'.

Glendrian – ruined croft

Glendrian village was situated on good grazing land in the centre of the ring. Today you can see the ruined houses and, also, one house that is still substantial. Plocaig is another ruined settlement. The Glendrian caves are to be found in a spectacular outward leaning headland. One cave is quite deep, a long crack in the cliff, but most are just overhangs.

1 Take the track, which climbs gently from the west end of the quarry. Keep right at the Y-junction and cross a deer fence at a kissing gate. The pleasing grassy track goes on into the centre of the Ardnamurchan Ring, and this is the place from where to look at the amazing circle of hills enclosing this grassy central area, with a lower ring inside it. Carry on to a burn, easy enough to cross in dry weather but the stepping stones have been disrupted and in spate it could cause a problem and you may have to paddle or return to the car park. Beyond the burn, fork right and ascend to explore some of the old ruined houses, part of the old settlement of Glendrian. Then follow a track along the hillside to a house, which still has a corner of roof and a section of the original tongue and groove panelling inside. Take care; the structure is not sound and you should just peep inside.

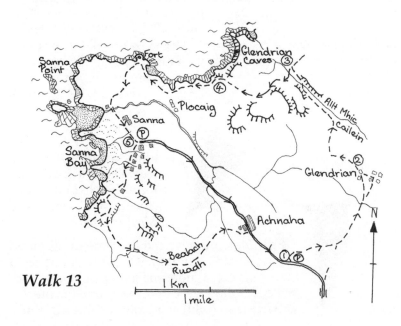

Walk 13

1 Km

1 mile

53

2 Then continue along the track through a gate gap in a wall. The path runs along the edge of the inner line of hills, then turns sharp right and goes through a narrow pass and over into Glen Drian, between the inner and outer rings of hills. As you go on, detour to the right over a rocky mound to avoid a very wet area. Then cross to the left and follow the path round into a very straight, narrow defile. This is quite wet in places, though in dry weather most bad bits can be avoided. Cross the burn on stepping stones. The path beyond has obviously been built up and gives pleasant walking through a narrow cleft in the rocks; then it turns away to the right.

3 At this point look for a faint path carrying on ahead and follow it as it winds down to the burn. Cross on convenient stones and go on ahead to pick up another faint path, probably an animal track, which winds round the base of a hillock to the left. Carry on along this path which skirts the bog until it converges with a deer fence. Round the corner there is a small gate. Go through, or over it if it is locked, and continue on the path, beyond it, skirting the bog, until this becomes very narrow. Cross it here, heading for a small cairn on a knoll on the far side. Carry on round the edge of the higher ground, over a low col and then you can either drop down and carry on round the edge, or go up and cross a shoulder. Both paths later converge. You are now heading for the sea. Cross a bog at a place where it is narrow, marked by two old stone rings, the base of shieling huts. Then climb up to the right to the top of a low hill, from where you have a superb view out to Rum, Eigg and Muck, and back along the coast to the fine headland of the Glendrian Caves. This is a good place to eat lunch and watch gannets and seals, and look for otters.

4 Go down the west side of the knoll on an increasingly clear animal track, heading for a fence corner. Ignore the gate through it, and, instead, follow the clear path round the outside above the low cliffs and bays of this delightful

Gannet

coast. Go past another gate, from where you can see the ruins of the settlement of Plocaig, over to the left beyond it. Wind right outside the fence and go round a tight corner; it is best to climb up onto a low rise here to avoid an overgrown wooded area. Bear right and come down to a fine white sand beach, with a dun beyond on a precipitous headland. Then turn west until you reach a cleft through the low hills and take the path through this, then round the far side to a house. Go down by its left side and cross a bridge to bring you onto the machair at Sanna. Walk along the track to the car park, where you may have left your second car.

5 To continue you may wish to walk back the 1¾ miles/3km up the road to the quarry car park, beyond Achnaha. Alternatively, if you have plenty of time, take the track running south behind the shore to the flat roofed Sanna Bheag. Walk across the turf in front of the house to a kissing gate, cross a burn and wind round uphill to another kissing gate. Climb the hill beyond on the pipeline track. At the top the path winds right and divides. Here take the left fork which contours round the hillside. Cross a burn and turn left to cross the low Bealach Ruadh, through the outer hills of the Ring. The view of the Ring from here is excellent. The path is waymarked with posts down the far side, crossing a bog and coming out on the road by a fence at the south end of Achnaha. Turn right to return to the quarry and your car.

Practicals

Type of walk: This is a fine interesting walk, mainly on paths, some of which are quite small, and there is one stretch where map reading is required (although there are animal tracks). It can be very wet in Glen Drian, and there are two burns which would be difficult or impassable in spate, so save the walk for a dry period.

Total Distances: 4½ mile/7.4km if two cars are used.
6½ miles/10.5km if you return from Sanna to Achnaha by road.
7½ miles/12.2km if you complete the full walk.
Time: 3 hours, 4½ hours, 5½ hours
Maps: OS Explorer 390 / Landranger 47

14

Portuairk and Sanna, Ardnamurchan

Park at the top of the hill above Portuairk in a badly signposted car park, grid ref 439679. To reach this, drive along the B8007, west, to pass through Kilchoan. Remain on the B-road for 3½ miles/5.5km, heading for Ardmurchan Point and Portuairk. Where it divides at Achosnich, turn right for Portuairk and carry on for ½ mile/1km.

Redpoll

The redpoll is a lively small finch. The male is dark brown in colour with a crimson forehead and crown. Its chin is black, distinguishing it from the linnet and the twite. The female has no red on its breast. The young have no red at all. In autumn and winter the redpoll consorts with siskins and tits and is to be seen and heard in alders and birches. In spring the male flies to and fro, trilling his simple love-song. When the birds are feeding or in flight they keep up a continuous twitter.

1 Turn right out of the car park and walk down the steep narrow single track road to a T-junction. The left turn leads to most of the houses that make up the little settlement of Portuairk. This walk turns right, just above the lovely shore, following a low carved sign directing you towards Sanna. Go past two houses and then take the signed green trod through birch. Cross the sandy burn on two metal bridges. Notice the sign that directs you up a narrow path, through rocks, above another small sea inlet.

Walk 14

Carry on through birch to pass through a gate in a fence above yet another sandy inlet. Drop down behind a cottage to come to a burn which you cross on large boulders.

2 Carry on winding slightly right round a large outcrop, where willow and oak thrive and where you might spot redpolls. Stroll on with bracken to your left. At the end of the glen the bog is covered with cotton grass and yellow flags. Ignore the first left turn and, a few steps along, take the good left turn, unsigned, up through bracken. Head on parallel with inland cliffs to your right. Walk on and then turn right up a stony gully, where you should wind from side to side to help your ascent. At the top of the gully bear left. Pause here to see a fine view of the island of Muck across the sea. Follow the clear path as it continues to climb steadily over peat and then a hillock. Then climb a ridge with a shallow very muddy gully to your left. Cross a damp area and, still curving left, pause at the top for a wonderful view of the glorious white sands of Sanna, the settlement and the many ribs of rock that run into the sea. Beyond several little islands, you can see the islands of Muck, Eigg and Rum. Descend to pass through a gate and move slightly right and cross a stream running through a shallow sandy ravine and walk on up the other side for another splendid view.

3 Go through a gate and then walk ahead across a green sward, with a boggy area and a flat roofed single storey house, beyond the bog, to your right. Then head for the shore. Go through a farm gate and walk right along the fine turf, above the sands of

57

the bay, with shallow dunes to your right. Join the shore and walk around the lovely bay. If the tide is high move into the shallow dunes.

4 Carry on around the bay, where you step across very shallow streams. Then step up onto an area of glorious turf to look into the next bay. Perhaps this is the place for your picnic. Then head on round the bay, on the dunes and up the riverbank, until you come level with a white house, with a blue door (at the time of writing). Cross the pedestrian bridge, over the river, to reach the right side of the house and walk on along a path. Where it becomes indistinct, climb up the grassy way, bearing half-left, and then straight up to the site of the fort on Rubha an Duin Bhain. The view from here is magnificent and this might be another choice for your picnic.

5 To return, descend to the footbridge and cross to join a grassy track that leads away from the shore. Join a reinforced track and follow it towards a car park. At the T-junction walk right, with several white cottages to your left. The track leads on well away from, but parallel with, the shore. After a boggy patch, colourful in June with yellow flags, leave the track and walk across the green sward to pass in front of the flat roofed single storey house, passed earlier, now to your left. Climb the path up the slope to the gate. Go on to cross the stream in the sandy gully. Follow the path uphill through another gate and on to the top of the hill until it divides into three. Take the middle one that runs down the little ridge.

Sanna Beach and Rum

6 Follow the path as it turns left and then descends the stony gully. Wind left along the grassy trod. Look out for a water hydrant and the manhole cover, and just before these, take the right branch and descend to cross the burn on rocks. Then retrace your steps to Portuairk. Climb the hill, left, to rejoin your vehicle.

Yellow Iris

Practicals

Type of walk: A really lovely walk. Best to wear walking boots

Total Distance: 4½ miles/7.4km
Time: 3 hours or more – as much as you can spare
Maps: OS Explorer 390 / Landranger 47

15

Kentra Bay and the Singing Sands, Ardnamurchan

Park at the end of the road at Arivegaig, grid ref 650677. To reach this, leave the A861, north of Acharacle, turning left onto the B8044. After just under a mile, turn left again and drive to the parking area, beyond a gate and before the wide bridge over the Allt Beithe.

The outward track on this walk is an **old drove road** once used for bringing cattle from the Small Isles to markets on the mainland.

The Beach, Camas an Lighe, at Gortenfern, is backed for a short way by low level sand dunes and if you walk close to these you might spot otter tracks, leading from the dunes to the sea. Behind the dunes the bay is edged with turf and heather and you can see an old croft and a barn. Deciduous trees arc round the bay and behind these stand the contrasting dark conifers. This is

The Singing Sands

a lovely sheltered corner of Ardnamurchan. It is a place where you will want to linger.

The Beach is also known as the **singing sands** of Gortenfern. You have to work hard with your shuffling boots across the dry sands, frightening the otters away, to make the grains sing!

1 Walk on from the parking area. Take note of the warning notice before you go through a side gate to cross the wide bridge over the river, hurrying to deposit its water into the sea. Continue on the good reinforced track with, to the right, the thrift-covered turf edging Kentra Bay where sheep feed. To the left are rocky outcrops, clad in trees and bracken. Follow the track as it winds right to cross a wooden bridge over the Allt a' Ghoirtein-eorna. Walk ahead towards tall metal gates and bear right before them, still edging the glorious bay, in the direction of 'The Beach and Ockle'. At low tide mud and sand stretch across this very wide part of the bay.

2 Follow the track as it winds left, away from the bay, and heads inland to a deer gate into Ardnamurchan Estate Forest, with another warning sign on the gate. Carry on the reinforced track as it passes through extensive plantations of conifers. As you go you might spot several four-spot chaser dragonflies. After nearly a mile from the deer gate look, on your left, for what looks like a quarry face, now well colonised with plants, and a track running off beyond it into another part of the forest. This is your return route.

3 Stroll on through conifers that now darken the way as they

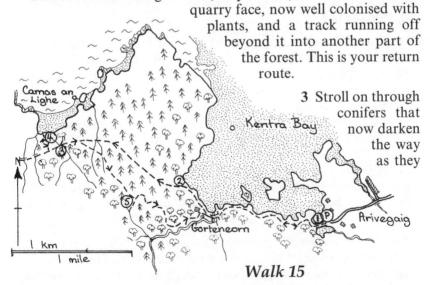

Walk 15

Four-spotted Chaser Dragonfly

crowd the immediate sides of the track. Continue on to an easy-to-miss signpost (it lies beyond the turn) and take the right turn for The Beach, Camas an Lighe. Drop down the very pleasant track, where in June wood warblers sing, to the shore at Gortenfern. Go quietly onto the sands as you might spot an otter disporting. Find a rock to sit on and enjoy the bird life. You could see terns, gannets, razorbills, guillemots and mergansers. Before you leave the beach, pause to take in the glorious view of the Small Isles.

4 Return up the path and turn left where it meets the main track. Continue through the dark stretch of conifers and a few steps beyond, take the grassy trod, going off right. If, after a short walk, a conifer is still lying across the way, blown down in the last gale, climb over the middle section of the trunk, where other walkers have gone before you. Dawdle on the pleasant way, where you might spot deer footprints and pine-marten droppings. Soon more fallen conifers lie across the track and, if they are still there, move left and wind round the tip of the trees – again where other walkers have beaten a path. A few steps further on there is another fallen tree and you can wind round its top quite easily.

5 After three-quarters of a mile from the start of this track, look for a 'fire prevention' notice at a junction of paths. Here wind left and descend the good track. Go through an open gate where the

woodland becomes deciduous and more open. Pass a house away on the left, with its ruined bothy on the right. Descend to a wide track and turn right. Walk on to pass through the tall gates ignored on your outward route. Beyond, continue on to cross the wooden bridge over the burn. Wind left, still on the track, and continue beside the bay. Notice as you go how the telephone posts carrying the power lines are embedded in the tidal narrows.

Otters

Practicals

Type of walk: This is a delightful walk on good tracks. First it takes you beside Kentra Bay and then ascends gently through the forest before dropping down to Camas an Lighe. The return is made on another pleasing track before continuing along beside the shore once again.

Total Distance: 6 miles/9.5km
Time: 3 hours
Maps: OS Explorer 390 / Landranger 40

16

Castle Tioram and the Silver Walk, Moidart.

Park in the car park for Castle Tioram, grid ref. 663720, which is at the end of the public road at Dorlin (Doirlinn). To reach this take the A861, north, from Acharacle, cross the bridge over the River Shiel and turn left onto a minor road. Follow this to its end.

Castle Tioram (Dry Castle) was an important centre for the Lords of the Isles. Its situation was ideal with a sheltered anchorage, easy access to west coast shipping routes and plenty of timber for ship building. It was probably built in the 13th century and then added to. It became a stronghold of the Clanranalds; but in 1693 the castle was seized by Government troops and held by them until 1715. Then the Clanranalds attacked and retook it but, in order to prevent it falling again into enemy hands, they burnt it.

To **visit the castle**, turn right out of the car park, heading towards it, along the path that follows

Castle Tioram

64

the shore in front of Dorlin Cottage. Cross the sandy causeway (**note** this is covered at high tide, even neap tides) to the island. The masonry is unsafe and you are asked not to go inside the ruins but can walk round the outside, except for the unsafe north wall, and appreciate its defensive position.

Eilean Shona is a large island in the mouth of Loch Moidart, joined to the smaller Shona Beag by a low neck of land. Shona Beag is a tidal island and there is a causeway giving access from the shore at low tide. Both islands are inhabited, but access is usually by boat.

1 From the car park, walk along by the beach which swings round to the right. Look for the clear but narrow path as it leaves the shore, passing into rhododendrons by the end of Dorlin Cottage garden. After a little way there is a metal gate in a fence, the start of the Silver Walk, with a notice warning people that they continue at their own risk as the path is dangerous. The gate is not locked; open it and continue, minding heads on the crossbar at the top (a danger for very tall people only). Go on along the path as it continues round the hill, climbing up and down steps. It is clearly not well maintained as it is quite overgrown in places and is slippery in wet weather, although it was well built originally when it was an estate path carved out of the hillside, 130 years ago. Follow it with care.

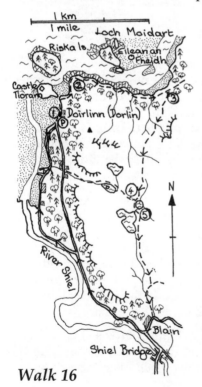

2 Go on round the point, from where there is a good view across to Eilean Shona and Shona Beag. Cross a section where the path has been built up with gabion baskets; this gets covered by the sea at extreme high tides and is slippery in consequence. Continue up the far slope and contour at a higher level where

Walk 16

the path has been cut out of the cliff in one place. Look across to Eilean an Fheidh, where red deer can sometimes be seen feeding. Divers and mergansers swim on the sheltered waters of the loch, and you may see an otter if you are lucky.

3 Cross two burns on well made stone bridges and then the path comes to a flatter boggy area, also with a burn; if the tide is low the best way is across the upper shore. Shortly after this, look for a small cairn on the right hand side of the path, marking the turning for Blain (the shoreside path continues up Loch Moidart). Turn sharply to the right at the cairn, leaving the Silver Walk, and head uphill; this path is boggy and braided but fairly clearly defined. Carry on climbing steadily up the hillside, making for a distinct saddle visible through the trees. Towards the top of the slope

Merganser

the path passes through the ruins of the old settlement of Briagh and then crosses a flatter area where it spreads and becomes less clear, reappearing as a good stalkers' path at the far side. Continue to the top of the hill, from where there is a good view across the small lochans to the hills between Acharacle and Salen. Then make your way down the hill to the shore of Lochan na Fola and follow the path round to the right.

4 Here, the path divides. If you wish to cut the walk short follow the branch round to the right and go on up the distinct valley away from the lochan. This takes you across a narrow col and down to a small reservoir; skirt this to the right and follow the path over the dam and down the valley. There are good views over to the Small Isles on clear days. The path brings you down to the road at the top of Dorlin, beside the red telephone box. Turn right and follow the road back to the car park.

5 This walk continues round the lochan towards a small stand of pine trees. Cross the two stiles over the fenced enclosure and stay with the well-marked footpath above Loch Blain, where you may

see red-throated divers. Stride the path through the valley of the Blain Burn from where there are more delightful views down across Acharacle and the lower end of Loch Shiel. Come down to a well maintained vehicle track which gives access to the radio mast on the hill; turn right and follow it down across the burn to the main road just beside the bridge over the Blain Burn. Turn right along the road until you reach a junction to 'Dorlin' and follow the road round beside the River Shiel, taking especial care on the blind bend just after the elegant arched foot-bridge, as the road is narrow here. After about a mile, take the estate track on the left along the bank of the river, which is deep, wide and fast flowing, with wooded banks; this traffic-free way gives pleasant easy walking. Continue past houses and then a boathouse as the river widens into its estuary. Where the track joins the public road at Dorlin, turn left and return to the car park.

Bog Asphodel and Sphagnum

Practicals

Type of walk: This is a very pleasing walk and is well worth the effort in spite of the state of the path round the point, where you do need to take care. You should wear waterproof footwear with good grips as the paths are slippery when wet. Do not attempt the walk at extreme high tide as one part of the path is often flooded under these conditions.

Total Distance: 6 miles/9.5km
Time: 4½ hours
Maps: OS Explorer 390 / Landranger 40

17

Ard Molich Woodland, Moidart

Park in the small car park, grid ref 717713, overlooking Loch Moidart. This lies beside the A861 between Acharacle and Kinlochmoidart.

Prince Charles Edward Stewart, Bonnie Prince Charlie, and six companions, were guests of MacDonald of Kinlochmoidart, while on their way to raise the Prince's standard at Glenfinnan. In commemoration of this visit seven beech trees were planted close to the loch and they were known as the **Seven Men of Moidart**. At the time of writing, sadly, only three trees survive.

Many **non-native trees** have been removed from Ard Molich Woodland to make way for the regeneration of a birch and oak woodland.

Loch Moldart, with Rum and Eigg

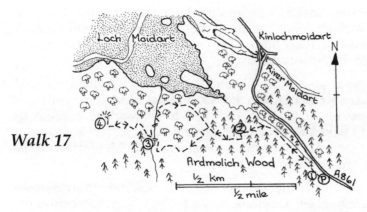

Walk 17

1 From the car park head along the well reinforced track into conifer woodland. Go on, downhill, crossing several small streams that have been culverted under the path. In late spring bluebells thrive along the edges of the ditches that keep the way well drained. The track then comes to a large stile over a deer fence, with a dog gate to its right. Beyond, carry on, soon to climb quite steeply to the first large boulder used as a route marker.

2 Wind on round a level stretch and then climb again. As you near the top of the slope, look for a very short grassy path leading into trees from where there is a splendid view of the head of Loch Moidart. Use your binoculars to look down on the mudflats where you might spot shelduck, greylag geese and mergansers. Return to the main rollercoaster path and follow it to reach a

Shelduck

69

Y-junction, marked with another large slab of stone. Take the left branch and continue along the high level way until the path descends to cross a burn, Allt Teang' Emilstain, where there is another similar waymarker.

3 Continue climbing steadily and then ascend wooden steps that help you over a large slab of rock. Follow the winding path as it continues on up and then, over high level moorland with a scattering of oaks, until you reach the end of the path at a viewpoint above more oak woodland. Look across Loch Moidart to see the 'Seven Men of Moidart'.

4 Then return over the open moorland to descend the steps down the huge boulder. Continue on to the path junction before the burn and turn left to descend a sloping path, with the burn racing down beside you. Cross on a bridge and go on down with the burn now on your left, shadowed by oak and birch. Here you might spot small green tiger beetles crossing the track as you go. Stroll on along a level way through an open area with a scattering of oak, rowan and birch. Eventually you arrive at the Y-junction reached at point 2 above. Bear left along your outward route and soon wind down to the first marker post you passed. Carry on down to the stile over the deer fence, then on climbing steadily to arrive at the car park.

Green Tiger Beetle

Practicals

Type of walk: A very satisfactory walk with some steepish climbs on a good track. The middle loop provides route options before these paths come together and you head west out on a spur to a hillock above oak woodland. From here you can enjoy spectacular views of Loch Moidart and the Small Isles.

Total Distance:	2½ miles/4km
Time:	2 hours
Maps:	OS Explorer 390 / Landranger 40

18

The Prince's Walk, Kinlochmoidart
with an extension to Loch nam Paitean

Park in a small area set aside for cars, grid ref 710727, just in front of St Finan's Church. This lies on the right side of the A861 half a mile north west of the bridge over the River Moidart.

St Finan's Church, set among trees, was constructed in 1857 and at that time it was the most northerly Episcopalian church. You might like to visit the charming, simple building before you start your walk.

The track, at the beginning of the walk, is bordered by **massive cypress trees**. As you continue along the track, notice the mature

Old Bridge, Kinlochmoidart

beech woodlands, which slope steeply up on the left. These form a dramatic backdrop to the magnificent baronial-style mansion. The house, Kinlochmoidart, was built sometime after 1593 when the land was granted to John MacDonald. It was destroyed in 1746 after the battle of Culloden. The present house was constructed in 1882.

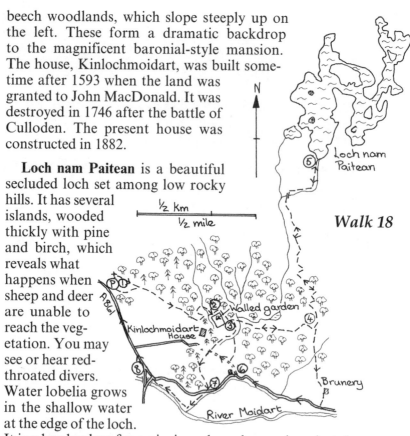

Loch nam Paitean is a beautiful secluded loch set among low rocky hills. It has several islands, wooded thickly with pine and birch, which reveals what happens when sheep and deer are unable to reach the vegetation. You may see or hear red-throated divers. Water lobelia grows in the shallow water at the edge of the loch.

It is a lovely place for a picnic and maybe a swim – but choose a midge-free day!

1 After visiting the church, return down the path and continue ahead on the signposted track, which passes under the giant cypresses. Carry on to go through a gate and soon follow the signed path, left, past outcrops of rock. The waymarks direct you left again through the woodland, climbing all the time, until the path winds sharply right, still ascending. The route is waymarked on almost every tree to help you along. Then the way winds a few steps left and just before a fence you go downhill. Ignore a muddy track and walk on the path up against the wall. Before you reach a ravine, wind right and follow the waymark directing you down a slope. Cross a narrow burn on stones, and descend a little to climb a waymarked ladderstile over a deer fence.

72

Water Lobelia

Continue down the slope with the deer fence now to your right. Go on down beside a wall and, near the wall corner, cross a ditch on a plank footbridge. It can be very wet here, so pick your way carefully.

2 Turn left and walk beside the wall with the ditch, in midsummer, covered with small purple and white flag irises. Where the wall turns away, cut off the corner on a little grassy path to climb a wire fence by a waymarked wooden stile. Wind round right and then left to edge a small wild garden and continue to a signpost.

3 If you wish to visit the loch as an extension to the walk, turn left, cross a bridge over the burn and go through a gate into the wood. The clear path winds up through a planted estate-woodland by the burn, past a pool and goes straight ahead across a slightly boggy area. Then it comes out onto open hillside. Go through a gate in a deer fence, which you must remember to close, and contour the hillside to cross another burn on a bridge and on to a T-junction, where you turn left.

4 The path climbs steeply through open birch woodland, with other deciduous trees. Soon it begins to zigzag which makes the gradient easier. It is a well-engineered stalkers' path, just a little worn in places. Above the trees it winds into a shallow valley, turning right at the top and crossing the burn on a culvert. Then it turns left again and follows the bank of the burn to the loch.

5 Return by your route of ascent until you reach the T-junction. Do not turn right here but carry on down the path to the foot of the hill, then keep left round the flat ground at the bottom. Go through a gate by a ruined building and on down the track to a gate out onto a public road. Turn right and walk along it for just under ½ mile/1km to a track beside a red painted cottage.

6 Turn right, through imposing gate posts, and walk up the track for 500ft/150m, past a cottage on the right to a waymark on the left where you rejoin the woodland walk by turning left down the lovely grassy track along the edge of the wood, named 'Mackenzie Walk'. Continue under more cypress trees and watch out for roe deer. Go through a gate to a narrow road.

7 Turn right and after 51yds/50m, take the arrowed gate on the left. Walk on under an avenue of lime and horsechestnuts. Go through another gate and turn right to walk a path beside the peat stained River Moidart, which is wide and shallow here. Stroll on under more cypress and Douglas fir to pass through a kissing gate. Here you might like to turn left to walk to the old bridge. It is now replaced by the modern bridge to your right.

8 Return over the old bridge and walk along the side of A861, using the verge. The road is quite narrow, but the traffic is generally light. After ½ mile/600m you turn right into the car park.

Roe Deer

Practicals

Type of walk: Generally easy walking on the low level ramble except for the climb through the wood, which though short, can be wet and slippery. The extension to the loch is steep and stony but follows a good clear path with some wet patches. Walking boots for the complete walk, a good idea.

Total Distances: Low Level walk 1½ miles/2.5km plus
                    extension adds an extra 3 miles/5km
Time: 1 hour + 2 hours
Maps: OS Explorer 390 / Landranger 40

NB If people want to do the woodland walk only, ignore the signpost to the loch and continue round the cut grass and down the drive, past the cottages to MacKenzie Walk.

19

Smirisary and White Sands Beach, Moidart

Park in a largish parking area, just before the end of the road, high above Smirisary, grid ref 653773. To reach this leave the A861 at Glenuig, heading west.

Domesticated **goats** have been escaping and becoming wild for many, many years. Escapees revert to the wild type within a few generations. Some goats have been deliberately set free to feed on lush grass on almost inaccessible ledges on cliffs, so removing the temptation for the less nimble sheep which can reach the ledges but be unable to get down, causing shepherds much tiresome effort in retrieving them.

1 Walk down the steep slope of the end of the road to take a signposted gate on the right, where a notice says that dogs are not permitted. Walk along the reinforced path

Eilean Shona from The White Sands

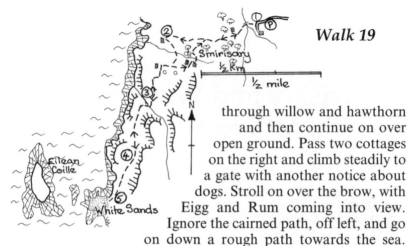

Walk 19

through willow and hawthorn
and then continue on over
open ground. Pass two cottages
on the right and climb steadily to
a gate with another notice about
dogs. Stroll on over the brow, with
Eigg and Rum coming into view.
Ignore the cairned path, off left, and go
on down a rough path towards the sea.
As you near an open area below inland cliffs you can see several
holiday cottages, all of which have been constructed from old
cottages of the deserted crofting village of Smirisary.

2 Turn left, before the picturesque cottages, along a path tucked up
below inland cliffs. Go on over a grassy area and then bear right
along a grassy trod and then a walkway, over a rushy bog, to
reach an inconspicuous sign directing you left 'for the white
sands'. Climb a low rocky bluff and walk its spine as it runs left
(south). There is a white cottage below to your right. At its end
go on to pass a roofless crofthouse. Just beyond, turn right along
a dry narrow path. Go through a purpose-built gap in a wall and
wind left with the path.

3 Stroll the easy way and follow it where it descends to cross a burn
on rocks, the stream tumbling on down to the sea through a steep
ravine. Once across, turn right as the way winds on round a large
boulder. Carry on and then head, right, up the easy-to-miss
smooth slope of another huge outcrop and carry on along a little
path. Then go on along a rather boggy way, where, in summer,
orchids, lousewort, milkwort, and water avens flower. Next, step
right onto the path as it traverses a narrow way, high above the
sea – children should be under control here.

4 Take care as you go over the next wet area, stepping from
boulder to boulder, where others have walked before. Soon you
have a glimpse of the lonely white sands ahead. As you wind

76

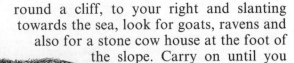

Wild Goats

round a cliff, to your right and slanting towards the sea, look for goats, ravens and also for a stone cow house at the foot of the slope. Carry on until you reach the lovely stretch of sand, much of it edged with fine greensward, where you will want to pause, dawdle or laze. Look for otter footprints and also for the cliffs of Eilean Shona with Ardnamurchan beyond, and a splendid view to Eigg and Rum.

5 Return along your same outward route, until you have reached the signpost 'to the white sands', then stride the duckboarding and follow the path through the rushes. Here go straight ahead across a pleasing greensward, cross a burn and climb gently to the right side of a greystone cottage. Beyond, a grassy trod leads up a short way, passes to the left of another cottage and then enters hazel woodland. The reinforced way is a joy to walk as it passes below birch, oak and hazel. It emerges from the woodland to cross a cairned open area to join your outward track at the cairn ignored almost at the outset of the walk. Turn right and retrace your outward route.

Practicals

Type of walk: The route down to Smirisary, and the return from it, makes a pleasing walk. The continuing way to the sandy beach is indistinct in places and often exposed, rocky and wet, but tantalising glimpses of deserted white sands encourage you to go on ahead.

Total Distance: 4 miles/6.5km
Time: 2 hours plus time spent on beach
Maps: OS Explorer 390 / Landranger 40

20

Rois-Bheinn (Roshven), Moidart

Park in one of the many parking places, on the sea side of the road between Alisary and Roshven. Most of the laybys are not surfaced but one is at about grid ref 734787. This is reached by turning left off the A830 onto the A861, west of Fort William, and travelling along the side of Loch Ailort.

Rois-Bheinn is a fine mountain, at 2866ft/882m. It is a Corbett but only just below Munro height, and the ascent is from sea level. Because of its position on the far end of a ridge it commands an unparalleled view of the western seaboard. As you look down on Loch Ailort and out to Eigg and Rum it is as if you are looking at a map, or an aerial photograph. The wall along its narrow summit ridge is beautifully constructed of stones standing on end. It is far too low to keep stock or deer in and must just be an estate boundary marker.

1 Walk south west along the road using the wide verge until

Perched Boulder, Rois-Bheinn

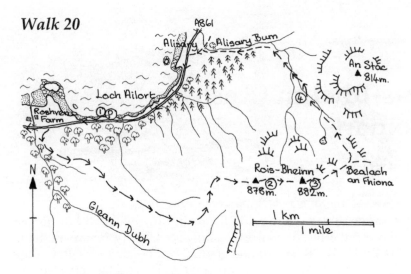

you go past the sign for 'Roshven'. Look on the left for a gate into the trees and go through. Turn right and make your way up the hill, which is boggy in places. Then wind round left and go through a gate in the higher fence. Follow a vague path up between birches and out onto open hillside. Work your way upward, heading for a large boulder, which has been visible from the road below. Beyond the boulder is yet another fence with a gate gap. Carry on upwards, choosing the driest route and working round right to a broad ridge. Stop from time to time to admire the superb view out to Eigg and Rum. Climb the ridge – you can go up more directly but it is quite steep; however the going improves as you get higher. On reaching a flat area, turn right to ascend easily to the summit, which is one of the ever-receding kind. There is a fine double cairn on the summit, and a magnificent view, all round, from Mull north to Ardnamurchan, Coll and Skye, with the Outer Isles beyond; inland hills stretch into the far distance.

2 Continue along the narrower ridge beside a low well-built wall, down to a dip and up to the next summit. This is higher than the western summit but only just; it doesn't look it and has a small insignificant cairn. If you don't want to tackle a steep descent, with a slippery section near the end, return by the way you came up.

Snow Buntings

3 Otherwise carry on beside the wall, down a small but distinct path to the Bealach an Fhiona between Rois-Bheinn and Sgurr na Ba Glaise. Keep left and go on down beside the wall, heading for the isolated rocky peak of An Stac. This part is very steep but there is a distinct path and it is dry and not too difficult. Go on down by the wall (and its associated old fence) into a corrie. Here there are various interesting rocks, in particular a splendid large perched boulder, and lower down a big rock split into two. Look for the base of a circular shieling hut.

4 Cross the burn after the wall has done so and then back again. The burn disappears into a gorge, but carry on down by the wall; the hillside is quite steep and wet in places. As it opens out you can see a conifer plantation below so head for its right corner. The hillside becomes wetter and covered in tussocky purple moor grass so proceed with care; you will find walking poles useful at this point. Then follow a small path to the fence round the plantation. Turn right, then left round the corner. The path continues all the way down, between the plantation and the birchwood in the river gorge below you. It is narrow and in places, exposed, and the upper part is overgrown with bracken, then purple moor grass again, so it is not easy and walking poles are useful again. Lower down the path leads into birches and improves. Go through a gap in a fence, onto a flat stony meadow, where, in summer, hardheads, devil's-bit scabious, hawkbit and eyebright grow. Join a track, which was the old way along the side of Loch Ailort before the road was made. Turn left and walk on to a gate out on to the main road. Turn left and return to your car.

Enjoy the fine views across the loch to Eigg. Look for herons and otters on the loch, and maybe a sparrowhawk in the woods. If it is getting towards dusk you might be lucky enough to see a wildcat.

Wild Cat

Practicals

Type of walk: A good climb although there are few paths and you need to be able to choose the best way. The route up is straightforward; the way down is steep and the lower bit above the burn, coming down to Alisary, could be unpleasant and slippery in wet weather. The views are superb.

Total Distance:	7–8 miles/11.4–13km
Time:	7 hours
Maps:	OS Explorer 390 / Landranger 40

Stalking is carried out on the estate, Roshven Hill, during September and up to October 21. For information about possible routes at this time tel: 01687 470215.

21a

River Callop Walk, Glenfinnan

Park in the Forestry Commission car park over the bridge, grid ref 924792. To reach this, leave Fort William by the A830, the Mallaig road. The turn for the car park is 2miles/3.4km before Glenfinnan.

The woodland about the River Callop is being restored to its original composition. Many of the pines have been there for a long time, but foreign conifers are being carefully removed. As you walk, look out for redpolls high in the trees, spotted flycatchers on lower branches, and grey wagtails by the river. Otters also occur along the river, and pine martens and wildcats live in the forest.

The attractive small butterfly, the **chequered skipper**, is gold or pale yellow with dark brown patterning.It is nationally rare, occurring in Britain only in this part of the Western Highlands in open oak woodland. It flies from May to July, and lays its eggs on the leaves of woodland grasses. The caterpillar spins the edges of the leaf together to form a protective shelter.

1 Leave the car park and turn right along the forest track, passing round the end of a gate. The forest opens out immediately to give a splendid view towards Glenfinnan;

Glenfinnan Monument

there are conifers to the left but open space down to the river on the right. As you continue the spruce crowd in but, after the first section, the way is shadowed by birch, pine, oak and rowan. Take the first small path, on the right, to reach a fine viewpoint above the River Callop, with a small lily lochan beside it. Then as you return to the main track, perhaps on a sunny day in late summer, look out for dragonflies, mainly Highland darters.

2 Continue along the track and take the next turn on the left. Climb a stile and then wind quite steeply to the top of a craggy knoll, crowned with dramatic old pine trees. There is another fine view from here of the head of Loch Shiel and Glenfinnan. Return to the track once more and carry on downhill to a bend with a large turning space on the right. Follow the waymarked path, beyond the space, to the top of another pine-clad knoll and another fine view.

3 Return to the track. A few metres farther on, just round the corner, is a new boardwalk under construction at the time of writing. This goes down to a bridge over the Callop just above its entry into Loch Shiel (the bridge is not yet constructed but it is hoped it will be in place by 2007). Follow the new path, and boardwalk beyond it, to the National Trust Visitor Centre where you may like to have tea and visit the Glenfinnan monument before returning by your outward route.

Walk 21a

Practicals

Type of walk: An easy walk on forest tracks and made paths, with some excellent views.

Total Distance: 4 miles/6.5km to the visitor centre and back
Time: 2–3 hours
Maps: OS Explorer 398 / Landranger 40

21b

Glenfinnan Circular, the Road to the Isles

Park in the pay-and-display National Trust for Scotland car park at the Visitor Centre, grid ref 907806. The car park lies on the right side of the A830 as you approach Glenfinnan from Fort William. There is extra car parking on the right on the west side of the River Finnan, grid ref 906808

Bonny Prince Charlie started his campaign, the Jacobite uprising of 1745, with just a few followers. He eventually commanded ten thousand ill-equipped and untrained men. With such a ragtag army he reached Derby and struck terror into the hearts of Londoners. But his followers were over-extended and Charles decided to retreat back north. This eventually led to the enormous slaughter at the battle of Culloden on 16 April, 1746, the end of the Jacobite cause and the clan system, and the final subjugation of the Highlands.

Glenfinnan Viaduct

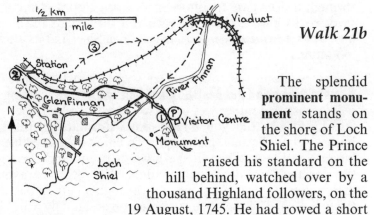

Walk 21b

The splendid **prominent monument** stands on the shore of Loch Shiel. The Prince raised his standard on the hill behind, watched over by a thousand Highland followers, on the 19 August, 1745. He had rowed a short distance up the loch from the house of MacDonald of Glenaladale on the western shore. The statue, erected in 1815 by Alexander MacDonald, is not of the Prince but an unknown Highlander who was one of those whose dedication to the cause 'fought and bled in that arduous and unfortunate enterprise'.

The Glenfinnan Station Museum lies beside the Fort William – Mallaig railway line. It tells the story of the construction of the line by Robert McAlpine, **Concrete Bob**, who was given this nickname for his use of concrete in the building of viaducts and bridges.

1 Leave the car park, cross the A-road with care, and walk right along the pavement. Cross the bridge over the River Finnan and then, in a few steps, turn left for Slatach. Stroll the leafy lane, ignoring tracks to dwellings on the right and the left. Where the lane swings sharp left, go ahead on a reinforced track, with a dwelling to the left. Carry on the easy-to-walk way, which is lined with colourful rhododendrons in spring, until you reach the main road once more.

2 Cross and turn right. After 200yds/175m along, take the signposted left turn rising to Glenfinnan Station. As you near the buildings, keep to the right of a railway carriage, used for holiday accommodation. Follow the signpost for 'woodland walk and viewpoint'. Descend steps and walk through the trees on a good track. Ignore the right turn and go on to cross a footbridge. Follow the continuing path as it winds left and up. Pass under the railway bridge on a pleasing cobbled way and then go

85

through a deer gate to climb on to open slopes, using a man-made rocky path. Follow the path as it turns right and climbs to a viewpoint from where you can see Loch Shiel and its attendant mountains.

3 Carry on along the rollercoaster way, which is marked with posts. Underfoot the peat holds much water and walking poles help across this rather wet traverse. As you go look for orchids and lousewort and you might spot whinchats on the top of bushes, 'chat-chatting' plaintively. To enjoy the incredible views – pause and look. Then the path winds round and down above the spectacular Glenfinnan viaduct. Follow the waymarker directing you down the slope and through a gate to pass below the first arch. The way then continues on and finally winds left to join a good reinforced track, where you turn right and stride on to join the main road. Turn left and use the verge to return to the car park.

Whinchat

Practicals

Type of walk: A delightful 2-mile walk with some magnificent views. The second part of the walk, over the open fell, can be wet underfoot, but there are plans in the offing, to upgrade it into a proper path, the work being done by the appropriate authorities.

Total Distance:	2 miles/3km
Time:	1½ hours
Maps:	OS Explorer 398 / Landranger 40

22

Arieniskill to Loch Beoraid, Morar

Park in a layby 110yds/100m west of the sign for Craiglea Guest House, grid ref 784832. To reach this, take the A830 west from Glenfinnan, to the end of Loch Eilt. The layby lies less than half a mile further on.

Prince Charlie's Cave, near the viewpoint, is one of the many caves in this area in which Prince Charlie is said to have spent the night after the disaster at Culloden. He covered a lot of ground, much of it very hard going.

Loch Beoraid is a remote loch, about 4 miles long, enclosed by high ground from all approaches from the south. It has spectacular high mountains round its head. The only low level approach is from Loch Morar, by way of Meoble, but this can only be accessed by boat.

Loch Beoraid

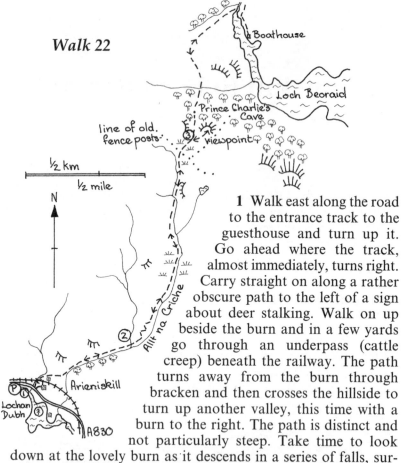

Walk 22

1 Walk east along the road to the entrance track to the guesthouse and turn up it. Go ahead where the track, almost immediately, turns right. Carry straight on along a rather obscure path to the left of a sign about deer stalking. Walk on up beside the burn and in a few yards go through an underpass (cattle creep) beneath the railway. The path turns away from the burn through bracken and then crosses the hillside to turn up another valley, this time with a burn to the right. The path is distinct and not particularly steep. Take time to look down at the lovely burn as it descends in a series of falls, surrounded by oak, birch and rowan. Look out, in summer, for stonechats and pipits, and common hawker dragonflies.

2 Higher up, cross a tributary burn by a step and go up a few zig-zags into a shallow valley. Here there is a peat-hagged area where the path becomes obscure; keep left for the easiest way. Aim for the path continuing up the hillside ahead, and go on up, over a lip into another valley. Beyond a wet stony area, there appears to be just a bowl of bog. But this is deceptive; continue by walking ahead, with a small burn to your right; there is a path and it is easily passable. Head for a cleft where the burn comes into the bowl, keeping to the left side of the cleft. The path goes up beside

88

the burn, crosses it on stones and comes out on a rocky knoll. Ahead is a line of old fence posts with an isolated ancient stile. Keep straight ahead then skirt round higher ground, to the left, into a small valley going down. Take a small path to the right, which climbs a rocky hill for a breath-taking view of Loch Beoraid in its hidden secluded valley. You can also see, down left, to the fields and woods of Meoble with Loch Morar in the distance. This is a wonderful place to sit for a while and well worth the climb.

Stonechat

3 Then return to the path in the small valley and follow it into the wood to search for Prince Charlie's Cave. After your explorations go back to the foot of the little path to the viewpoint. Then retrace your outward route, enjoying as you go, the views down Loch Ailort and across to An Stac, with Rois-Bheinn behind it and Sgurr na Ba Glaise to the left. Go through the cattle creep, below the railway line, and then along the road to your car.

Practicals

Type of walk: This is a fairly easy climb up a pleasant valley to a superb viewpoint. The path is good in the valley but becomes obscure in places higher up and care must be taken with navigation. It would not be a good walk for misty weather for this reason and, because the object of the walk is the view and the visit to the cave.

Total Distance: 3½ miles/5.8km
Time: 3 hours
Maps: OS Explorer 398 / Landranger 40

NB Stalking takes place on the Glen Mama estate during September and October; contact number 01687 470207. This will not affect the walk as the path is an official right of way.

23

Peanmeanach, Ardnish

Park in the layby, grid ref 743836, beside the new A830, Fort William to Mallaig, north of Loch Dubh (between Lochailort and Loch nan Uamh). This lies 16 miles/26.5km west of FortWilliam.

Loch nan Uamh is where Prince Charles Edward Stewart landed with six companions on July 25, 1745. A month later he raised the standard at Glenfinnan and the rebellion began. In September 1746, after defeat and months of trekking and hiding, he finally left for France, again from Loch nan Uamh. There is now a cairn by the loch to commemorate this.

Peanmeanach, once a small settlement, is now a row of ruined cottages standing above a most beautiful sandy beach. The only way the inhabitants or visitors could reach it, was by boat or by

*Peanmeanach
and Rois-Bheinn*

traversing the path taken on this walk. One of the cottages has been restored and is now used as a bothy.

1 Leave the parking layby by the path, flagged with a Scottish Rights of Way sign, going downhill away from the road. The path runs along beside a fence with scrubby woodland on the other side and winds round the base of a small hill to come beside the railway line. Wind left following the line to the beginning of Loch Dubh, visible through the trees. Cross the railway on a substantial arched bridge and then go over the burn beyond on a footbridge.

2 Head away, on the path, from the railway, through a mixture of open land and scrub. The distinct way then takes you over a small rise and on across a boggy area to ford a narrow burn. Walk on for 220yds/200m and then follow the path as it climbs steeply through scattered trees and up slabs of rock. Eventually the angle of the way eases and finally the path emerges onto a high shelf above Loch nan Uamh, with superb views out towards Rum and Eigg beyond Arisaig.

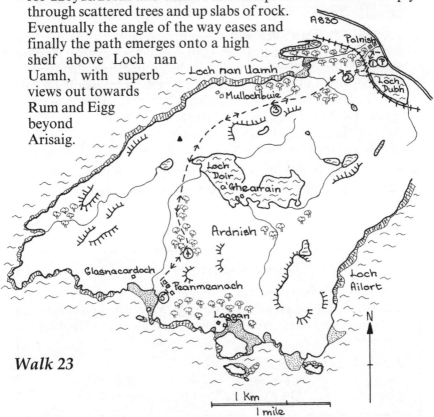

Walk 23

3 Carry on along the almost level path for over 1mile/1.5km. The way then crosses a low rocky rise and winds round the end of Loch Doir'a'Ghearrain where, in the summer you might look for red-throated divers. Go on down a small valley and cross the outflow burn, which wanders across a widening boggy valley. The path continues, skirting the edge of the bog, below steeper ground, and then bears left through a delightful small oak and birch wood. Eventually you arrive at a large flat expanse of bog across which the ruined cottages at Peanmeanach can be seen.

Terns

4 Turn right beside a ditch and follow the straight clear path across the bog, which is much drier than you would expect. As you approach the shore of Loch Ailort the ground rises slightly and becomes dry and grassy. There are several remains of the cottages of Peanmeanach here, including a bothy, which is in good repair. The beach is a glorious curve of sand, backed by the short flowery turf. Terns fish, oystercatchers call, and if you wait quietly you may see an otter.

5 You will want to pause on this lovely peaceful shore before retracing your steps across the high peninsula, enjoying the views in reverse.

Practicals

Type of walk: In spite of the low boggy areas interspersed between the higher ground, a distinct path (rough in places and sometimes wet) takes you all the way from the A-road to a fine sandy beach.

Total Distance: 8 miles/13km
Time: 4 hours
Maps: OS Explorer 398 / Landranger 40

Borrodale to Scamadale, and Arisaig

Park in Arisaig, near the Spar shop, grid ref 659864. If using two cars, there is room for one or two cars to park near Borrodale Farm on the corner where a track leaves the A830, grid ref 695849. Or you could take the Shiel Buses bus which leaves Arisaig at 9.20 a.m and get off at Borrodale Farm. Alternatively get someone to drop you there. Access to Arisaig is by the A830, Fort William to Mallaig road, then turn down into Arisaig.

Mallaig lies 31 miles north-west of Fort William on the A830. It connects with Armadale on the Isle of Skye. It is the end of the road, the 'Road to the Isles', and the western terminus for the Jacobite steam train. South-east of the town is Loch Morar, Britain's deepest freshwater loch, which plunges 1017ft/311m. It has a monster, nicknamed Morag.

1 Go through the gate opposite the entrance to Borrodale House, following a Scottish Rights of Way Society sign to 'Arisaig, 8 miles'. Cross the field to a gate into the wood at the top, marked with a 'Walkers Welcome' sign and information

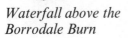

Waterfall above the Borrodale Burn

93

about deer stalking. Go through the wood (much overgrown with rhododendrons) and come out at the top, then follow the wood round left to the corner of a deer fence where there is a gate. Go through and turn left. Do not follow quad bike tracks. The path at the time of writing is indistinct here; the best thing to do is follow the line of the Borrodale Burn, keeping well above it. Ahead the burn makes a big bend so head for this and go round the outside of it. Here the path becomes distinct once more, climbing in zigzags up along the edge of the narrow gorge in which the burn now flows. Step across two tributary burns and continue climbing. At one point there is a fine waterfall on a tributary on the other side.

2 After about two miles the path levels out and runs through a valley, then suddenly turns left and fords the Borrodale Burn. The crossing of the burn here could be difficult if it is in spate. If so try 110yds/100m further on and cross, making use of some small islands. Climb up beside a tributary burn to Lochan a'Bhealaich, not far above the valley you have just left. Follow the path round left above the shore, then carry on in the same general direction, contouring, with steep slopes to the right and a wide empty valley below. Keep high, do not be tempted to go downhill. Cross the face of the hill and then bear right into the next big valley and walk up it to cross an ancient deer fence to reach the col at the top.

3 Go straight ahead, soon crossing to the left side of the valley with the little burn, the Allt Mhic Keillig, to your right (do not cross

Wheatear

this burn in spite of other confusing paths). The path becomes boggy but is marked with old cairns. Watch out for a large cairn where the path turns left over a low col, leaving the valley of the small burn and going steeply down a pleasant grassy bank. Then carry on down beside another burn, the Allt an Eas Bhain; although the path is steep and wet in places the direction now is fairly obvious, and there are new cairns in place.

4 Cross a stile into a small plantation and then go on down a ride until the path emerges onto a track to the left of a cottage at Scamadale. All the way down this long descent there are excellent views over Loch Morar. Turn left on the track and walk, easily, through birch and oak woodland over a low hill and down the far side, then skirt the wooded hill with a huge area of bog stretching away to your right. Here you might disturb a snipe probing the mud for prey.

Walk 24

Spotted Flycatcher

5 Cross the level crossing over the railway, then continue on the reinforced track to Kinloid, where the surface becomes tarmacked. Cross the new main road and go straight ahead. At the old main road turn left down into Arisaig.

Practicals

Type of walk: This is a strenuous walk and requires some route finding ability in places, although most of the route is clear and well marked with cairns. At the time of writing the construction of a new road is beginning to the south of Arisaig and it is not clear where it will go in relation to this walk. However since the route is a right of way there will be a way to cross the road.

Total Distance:	8 miles/13km
Time:	5–6 hours
Maps:	OS Explorer 398 / Landranger 40

The contact number for stalking is 01687 450609.

25

Arisaig to Camas Ghaoideil

Park in the large parking area opposite to the Spar shop in Arisaig, grid ref 659864. Arisaig is reached by taking the A830 west, for 29 miles, from Fort William.

From Arisaig there are wonderful views across to the islands of Rum and Eigg. The **Land, Sea and Islands Exhibition Centre**, set in a derelict bothy, now restored, is well worth a visit.

The stream from Loch nan Eala was **canalised** to allow logs to be floated downstream from the sawmill to the shore.

Cup-and-ring markings found on the boulder, close by the path, might have been a pre-historic system of waymarking,

Cup-and-ring marked stone

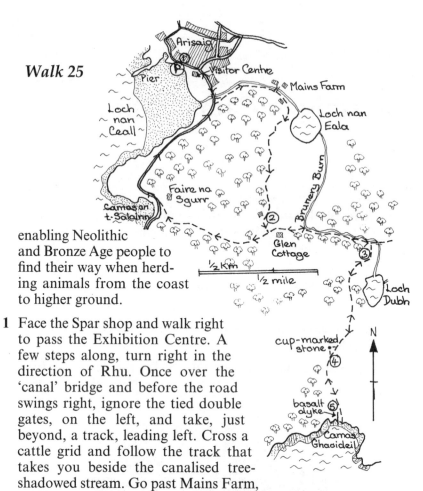

Walk 25

enabling Neolithic and Bronze Age people to find their way when herding animals from the coast to higher ground.

1 Face the Spar shop and walk right to pass the Exhibition Centre. A few steps along, turn right in the direction of Rhu. Once over the 'canal' bridge and before the road swings right, ignore the tied double gates, on the left, and take, just beyond, a track, leading left. Cross a cattle grid and follow the track that takes you beside the canalised tree-shadowed stream. Go past Mains Farm, a fine stone house, with outbuildings and a chimney, the remains of the mill. Continue ahead through a gated farmyard and then walk out into the open glen, with Loch nan Eala (loch of the swans) to the left. Continue on along the winding track.

2 At Pheasantry Cottage, curve round with the track and, a short distance along, at a cross of tracks and in sight of Glen Cottage (a white painted house), turn left again to walk a track in front of the dwelling. Go through two gates over the track into fine woodland with a gurgling stream to your left. Here you might spot a heron. At the top of the slope take, on the right, a large wood and metal gate.

98

3 Walk on along a rising track through birch. Then Loch Dubh (black loch) comes into view. In June look for water lilies edging the lovely pool. They grow far enough from the shore to be out of reach of the deer but in shallow enough water for the plants to take root. Carry on the glorious way to pass through a deer gate and go on across the valley, keeping to the right of a muddy section of the path. Then as the way begins to climb, look for the cup and ring boulder, among rushes on the right, a few steps away from the path.

4 From here the pleasing grassy track leads to a fallen beech. Some of its roots are still in the ground and the foliage is thriving. Continue on the path to the top of the hill and enjoy the splendid view down to a charming bay, Camus Ghaoideil. To descend, move right for a few steps to pick up a grassy swathe, through bracken from where, in summer, stonechats call, which leads down to the beach. Or you may prefer to sit by the basalt dyke, also on the right, and spend time watching for otters.

5 Then begin your return by retracing your steps to Glen Cottage. Here go ahead at the cross of tracks, just beyond the house, and follow the good track until you reach the narrow road to Rhu. Here walk right and continue to Arisaig, with glorious Arisaig Bay to your left.

Heron

Practicals

Type of walk: A really delightful walk, along good tracks at first and then over mainly grassy trods, which lead you over a hill and then down to a remote delectable bay.

Total Distance: 5½ miles/9km
Time: 3 hours
Maps: OS Explorer 398 / Landranger 40

26

Rhu and Port nam Murrach, Arisaig

Park opposite a jetty in a space at the end of the public road, grid ref 627852. If this is full there is a good space on a bend 425yds/400m farther back. To access this drive the minor road from Arisaig along the south side of Loch nan Ceall, signed Rhu.

A **gannet** is wonderful to watch. It is a large, startlingly white bird, with obvious black wing tips. Its wing span exceeds six feet and carries the bird lightly and high above the waves as it watches for fish below the water. The dive for its prey may start a long way up in the air. With half closed wings it shoots down obliquely, then, closing its wings it plunges arrow-like into the water, with a splash. Its prey is swallowed under the water and then the bird reappears, flapping heavily for a few yards before it catches the breeze and sweeps easily upward.

Port nam Murrach

1 Go through the gate ahead and along the continuing stony track. Pause to enjoy the stunning views out to Eigg and Rum, and to Skye, over Arisaig's myriad islets and skerries adorned with white sand beaches. Go through a small gate beside a deer gate and walk on as the track swings left. Ignore a grassy track going off to the right and carry on along the edge of a straight valley, heading south. Bear right before a house called the Steadings and cross a small col towards Rhue House.

2 Just before its cattle grid turn left, following a waymark on the gatepost, to cross below a shed and go down a sheltered path between a fence and a low turf and stone wall, set with wind-pruned trees. Follow the path to edge two sides of a field; then bear left to a gate. Go with the well-trodden path as it continues along the drier edge of a boggy valley. Head on as it approaches the coast, then wind left and climb slightly to pass through a gate gap in a wall. Drop down rocky steps, before descending the lovely grassy sward beyond, to a delightful white sand beach, Port nam Murrach. Here you will want to spend some time. There are islands and rock pools and a fine view over to Ardnamurchan. Out on the rocks, at the end, you are looking directly across to Eigg, with Rum behind. On a breezy day gannets

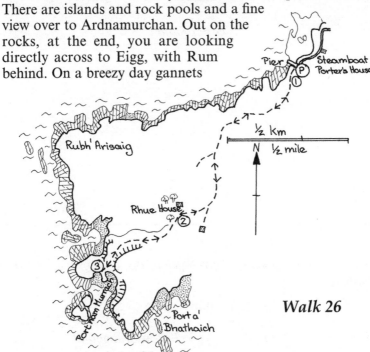

Walk 26

101

plunge into the water just offshore and manx shearwaters, terns and kittiwakes fly past. You may see great skuas harrying them for their fish.

3 When you have stayed awhile, return to your car by your outward route.

Great Skua

Practicals

Type of walk: A good path for much of the way, with very little climbing.

Total Distance: 2½ miles/4km
Time: 2 hours
Maps: OS Explorer 398 / Landranger 40

27

Bracorina to Stoul, Morar

Park at the end of the road, grid ref 725927, at Bracorina. There is limited parking on the right side and you are asked not to block the turning space. To reach this drive south from Mallaig on the A830, take the left turn beyond the River Morar and wind back towards Morar, crossing the river again. Then take the right turn just beyond the river to Bracora and Bracorina. Drive east for 3 miles.

The Morar estuary is surrounded by beaches of dazzling white sand, formed of weathered quartzite. The village of Morar huddles along the railway line in a dip in the hills north of the estuary. Loch Morar is the deepest in Britain – 1017ft/311m.

1 From the parking area walk on a few steps and head left up the slope to climb a ladderstile, where a signpost states that Stoul is

Stoul and Loch Nevis

Walk 27

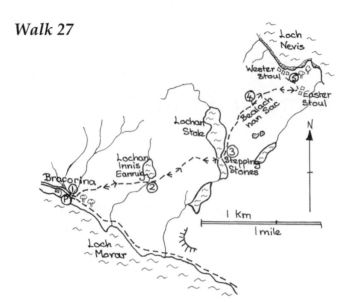

2½ miles. Continue up the stony and often wet path to climb the next ladderstile and go on through open oak woodland. Go over the next stile and continue on up the well cairned way. Cross two narrow hill streams with a step and carry on up, the way quite tough but never in doubt.

2 Stroll on along the right side of Lochan Innis Eanruig; in early summer its surface is white with water lilies and here bog bean grows. Ascend the continuing rough path, keeping to the right side of a boggy area, below a small cliff on your right. At the top of the gentle slope, where the path seems to divide, keep to the left branch. At the brow look back on an interesting view of Eigg, with Rum behind. Carry on, following the cairns as they wind down towards Lochan Stole, which you cross on stepping stones. If the stones are under water and you feel unable to cross, this will be the point of return with, ahead of you as you go, fine views of the vast Loch Morar to your left after you pass the small lochan.

3 Once across the stepping stones, climb the short steep pull uphill and then follow the path as it contours above Lochan Stole. Pass a small circular wall, probably an old shieling, and climb gently to the top of the Bealach nan Sac. Pause here to admire the

magnificent view; there is a steep drop to Loch Nevis and across the loch nestles Inverie at the end of the long ridge from Ladhar Bheinn. Up beyond the narrows, Sgurr na Ciche dominates the landscape.

4 Then drop down the very steep path towards Stoul. It is still cairned but not as clearly as on the way up so take care not to lose the way. Go through a gap in a turf and stone dyke into the ruins of the settlement of Easter Stoul where there are the remains several buildings. The track all but disappears into a series of sheep tracks but make your way down to a gate in the fence above the left corner of the settlement. From here you can get down to the beach and the ruins of Wester Stoul. The splendid view up the loch is enhanced by the wooded headland of Torr nan Gamhainn.

5 Then return by the same route.

Raven

Practicals

Type of walk: Though this is a long hard linear walk, you are amply rewarded by some spectacular views.

Total Distance: 6 miles/9.5km
Time: 3–4 hours
Maps: OS Explorer 398 / Landranger 40

28

Glasnacardoch to Loch Eireagoraidh, and Mallaig circular

Park in a wide, deep 'layby', grid ref 675957, on the right side of the B8008, just beyond the footpath sign on the right. If travelling from the south towards Mallaig, on the A830, the well signposted B-road, for Glasnacardoch, goes off right, a mile before the end of the A-road.

The A830 from Fort William to Mallaig is often called the **Road to the Isles**. It ends at Mallaig where the hills drop suddenly to the sea and grey buildings cluster round the busy harbour.

Inverness and North Argyll were chosen by Bonnie Prince Charlie as being the most likely areas to support his cause as they had long been centres of Catholicism. The remote peninsulae between Mallaig and Lochaline are closely

An Leth-Allt and Carn Mhic a' Ghille-chaim

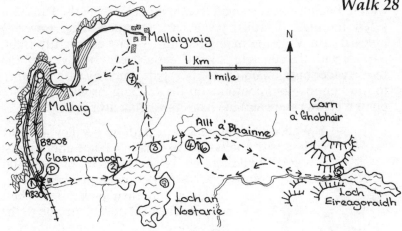

connected with the **1745 rebellion**. Many clansmen from Knoydart, Morvern and Ardnamurchan fell at Culloden.

1 Turn left from the parking area and descend the B-road to take the signposted footpath on the left. Walk the reinforced track, pass under the railway line and, where the track swings left to a large white dwelling, go ahead through a metal gate with a notice saying 'all dogs on leads and no vehicular access'. On the left of the gate is a tiny green triangle with the letters FP on it. Go past some very old cottages with tin roofs. Opposite, in the right season, look for ragged robin, spearwort and flags. Go on along the occasionally boggy path, with sleepers over the worst patches. Follow the waymarked posts to come close to Loch an Nostarie, where you might spot red throated divers. Continue on the path above the shore bearing steadily left to a tall stile over the deer fence.

2 Beyond, walk on to the next waymark above the loch. Cross a small stream on stones and go on climbing towards the next waymark. Then walk on up to a three-armed signpost embedded on a little hillock, standing proud in this lonely corner of moorland, with hills and rocky outcrops all around.

3 Walk on in the direction of Loch Eireagoraidh. The rather wet path passes through bog myrtle, lousewort, cotton grass and dark blue milkwort as it follows the line of a pipeline from the

107

loch. It is marked with small concrete posts, the first ones topped with red paint. Cross a small stream and climb gently. Pause for a few minutes to look back at An Sgurr on Eigg, towering upward in a V of the mainland hills. Carry on slightly right, parallel with the concrete posts. Cross a stream on a sleeper and then a wider burn on boulders (if in spate you may wish to return to the signpost and continue on the Mallaig circular walk, see point 6 below) and continue to go through a deer gate.

4 Walk half right on a clear path up a valley, keeping in line with the posts. Step over a fence and go past a small building and 'bits and pieces' of the water pipeline. Cross a wet patch just beyond the building and then pick up the best route to the next post. Carry on to the right side of a bog, keeping to the base of slightly higher ground. Join an indistinct path bearing left over hummocks of moorland and then follow a much clearer way as it climbs beside a tumbling burn carrying water from the loch above. Enjoy the pretty waterfalls as you progress. Go on through a ravine overlooked by Carn Mhic a' Ghille-chaim, with two perched boulders, one on either side of the dramatic trench. Carry on up the path to a water tank and then, where the path almost peters out, cross a broken fence, right, and clamber over boulders to come to the side of the loch's small dam. Wind round left for a good sheltered rock seat for a picnic and, if you are lucky, time to watch the antics of grey wagtails and dippers.

*Fragrant and
Lesser Butterfly
Orchids*

5 Return by the same path through the deep cleft, with the rocky hillsides on either side. At another water tank go on ahead (ignore a trace of a path that goes right) and wind up and round the pathless hillside to a derelict fence and an isolated gate. Cross the fence and bear away left to return to the bank of the river, where a better path runs beside a fence with the river foaming down falls and waterslides on your left. Cross the fence and follow a tiny path as it winds round the hillside, more or less parallel with, and below the fence, which soon disappears. Bear gradually right. When you come over a rise and see a deer fence below you, turn right to climb and then contour, following animal tracks, above the deer fence until you come to the gate used earlier (see end of point 3).

Marsh Marigolds and Water Avens

6 Go through and return by your outward route to the signpost. Turn right, signed 'Mallaig Circular', and follow the clear path across the hillside and along the lip of a small gorge. Cross the burn at the top of the gorge and go along beside a deer fence to a gate. Turn right to go through the gate and then walk straight ahead up a boggy valley to another deer gate. Beyond, the way is drier. Look out for orchids in the flushes in June. You might spot at least five species, including lesser butterfly and fragrant orchids.

7 Cross the col at the valley head and then climb left, following waymarked posts. Contour round above a large valley above Mallaigvaig, with fine views over Loch Nevis and the Sound of Sleat. The small rough path comes to a metal gate in a fence and then joins a well made path at a signpost. Turn left and walk down the path into Mallaig. As you go, if in late spring or summer, look out for globe

109

flowers, water avens, valerian and primroses. Between two seats the path turns right and descends, now paved, between gardens to the road. Turn left and walk round the bay. Opposite the tourist information office, turn left onto the B8008, to Glasnacardoch, and follow this back to your parking area. As you go you might hear grasshopper warblers in the scrub below the road.

Grasshopper Warbler

Practicals

Type of walk: The whole walk, as written above, is quite tough in parts. You might prefer to make it into two. For an easier and shorter walk, turn left at the signpost or, for a longer one to the loch, return from the signpost by your outer route.

Total Distance:	Complete walk 7½ miles/12km
	There and back, returning by the same
	route 6 miles/9.5km.
	Circular walk 3½ miles/5.5km
Time:	4 hours. 3 hours. 1½–2 hours
Maps:	OS Explorer 398 / Landranger 40

Guirdil, Rum

Caledonian MacBrayne ferries sail from Mallaig to Rum. For information on days and times of sailings tel: 01687 462403 or visit www.calmac.co.uk. MV *Shearwater*, Arisaig, also visits Rum. For information on times of sailing and time spent on the island etc tel: 01687 450224.

On Guirdil beach look for pebbles of **bloodstone**, pale green with red spots. Bloodstone is fashioned quite easily and was probably used for arrowheads in Stone Age times. Flint stone was scarce in the Highlands and bloodstone was a good substitute. Artefacts have been found on the isle of Eigg, Skye and Ardnamurchan, most likely brought by prehistoric traders from Rum.

Towards Guirdil from Shellesder

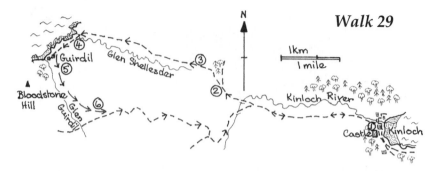

In 1845 Hugh Miller walked over the **hills to Guirdil**. He wrote of the village 'All was solitary. We could see among the deserted fields the grass-grown foundations of cottages razed to the ground; the valley had not a single inhabited dwelling. It seemed as if man had done with it forever.'

In 1845 the **2nd Marquis of Salisbury**, bought the island for £26,455. He restocked Rum with red deer. He built a pier and tracks were made to Kilmory and Harris. A quarry was opened up on Bloodstone Hill, from which Queen Victoria would eventually receive a coffee-table top of polished bloodstone.

1 Leave Kinloch Castle and set off northwards. Turn left before the bridge over the Kinloch River. Continue through alder woodland to your right and conifers to your left. Through the latter you might spot Hallival and then, nearer, the ridge of Barkeval. Pass through the deer fence by a tall gate or the equally tall kissing gate, leaving the trees behind. After two miles from the castle, the rough stony way divides. Take the right fork and press along the rough way. Look right towards Kilmory Bay for a dramatic view of Skye. Cross two burns by small bridges.

2 After just over ½ mile/1km, look for the narrow way which climbs left, the springy turf a great relief after the stony track. Follow the path to continue above a small fenced area of woodland. Here, at the right time of the year, you might hear a cuckoo calling. The path climbs steadily into the heart of the hills.

3 Once over the highest part you begin a gradual descent into Glen Shellesder. Step across several streams and look for red damselflies about the water, and also for two species of sundew, the long-leaved and the round-leaved. Go on descending.

4 Follow the path as it swings south west, from where there is a wonderful view of the isle of Canna. Cross the Shellesder Burn by convenient stones above a little waterfall and walk on. Press on, now climbing steadily above many lazy-beds, used by the inhabitants of Guirdil before they were 'cleared'. Step over the next burn and go on uphill beside an old turf and stone dyke to your right. Here you might like to pass through the wall and descend the path to the site of Guirdil and the beach.

5 Then return up the path to the decrepit wall and follow it right, keeping above and parallel with the Guirdil River. Look across to see an enclosed area of woodland. Stroll on beside the wall. Here you might spot feral goats on the slopes. Follow the narrow path beside the wall into Glen Guirdil, to pass the foundations of two enclosures on your right. Here the glen is overshadowed by towering steep-sided Bloodstone Hill, and here ancient man found stone hard enough for crude tools and weapons. Where the wall ends, begin to bear slightly left over the wet tussocky turf until you reach the side of a tributary burn. Here in the shelter of the ravine, grow many rowans, in early summer laden with creamy white blossoms, together with several aspens, with leaves pleasingly quivering. In summer roseroot flowers about the many delightful waterfalls.

6 Proceed ever upward, stepping across narrow streams, to join a path coming up from the foot of Bloodstone Hill. Turn left on the path and go on climbing to the Bealach a'Bhraigh Bhig, from where there is a tremendous view to Sanday and, ahead, to the Red and Black Cuillin of Skye. Follow the good path over the pass. Then drop down across the flatter area about the stream,

Cuckoo

the Abhainn Monadh Mhiltich. This path, wet in parts, leads to Malcolm's Bridge, where you turn left onto a landrover track. Go past the remains of Lord Salisbury's dam and, joining your outward track at the forked junction, carry on to Kinloch.

Canna from Rum (near Guirdil)

Practicals

Type of walk: This is a long, hard walk, which will be enjoyed by seasoned fell walkers. The paths can be rough and wet. The pathless area needs care when crossing the tussocky grass. If after rain some of the burns are impassable or bridges are down be prepared to turn back and retrace your steps.

Total Distance: 12 miles/19km
Time: 8 hours
Maps: OS Explorer 397 / Landranger 39

Dibidil, Rum

For details on how to reach Rum see walk 29

The **bothy at Dibidil** is a restored crofthouse for use by anyone wishing to stay overnight on the far south-east of Rum. Close by are the ruins of other crofthouses and collecting pens, an idyllic corner in the afternoon sun. From the grassy sward in front of the bothy you have a dramatic view of the slopes of Askival, Trollaval, Hallival and Ainshval cradling the glen, with Sgurr nan Gillean directly behind the bothy.

If you walk down towards the bay you might hear the hundreds of **Manx shearwaters** that float on the water and chatter. After dark they return to their burrows and their solitary young, high on the mountain tops. They nest in burrows in turf, in cracks or caves in rocks or among the debris of scree and fallen rocks. For centuries it was the common practice of the inhabitants of Rum to harvest these birds for food from the mountain top colonies.

1 Leave Kinloch Castle and walk right (south) to pass the reserve office. Go on along the continuing track through pleasing woodland to pass through magnificent white gates. Walk

Manx Shearwaters

115

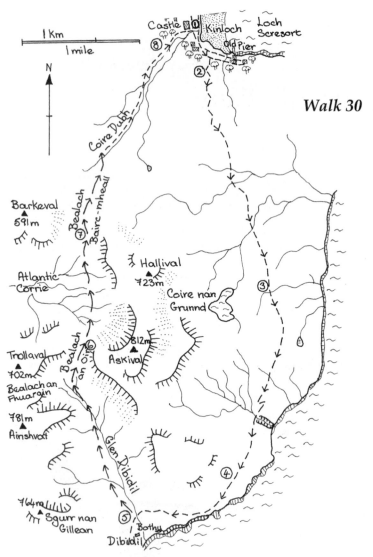

1 Km

1 mile

N

Castle Kinloch
Loch Sresort
⑧
Old Pier
②

Walk 30

Coire Dubh

Barkeval
591m

Bealach
Bairc-mheall

⑦

Hallival
723m

Atlantic
Corrie

Coire nan
Grunnd

③

Bealach
na Oir

⑥
812m
Askival

Trollaval
702m

Bealach an
Fhuarain

781m
Ainshval

Glen Dibidil

④

764m
Sgurr nan
Gillean

⑤
Bothy
Dibidil

on to take the signposted right turn for Dibidil along a stony
path. Follow it as it leads steadily upwards through heather
moorland. Look for the great flat outcrops of rock, used as anvils
by hoodie crows and gulls for smashing cockles and mussels.

2 As you climb through small birches, rowan, shrub willow and
alder the view behind you unfolds, with Loch Scresort and

Waterfall, Allt-nam-Ba

Mulloch Moor beyond. As you reach the top of the slope the isle of Eigg gradually comes into view across the Sound of Rum. First you see the craggy side of Beinn Bhuidhe and then the huge distinctive top of An Sgurr. Beyond lie the mainland mountains. Then you reach a deer gate and realise that from now on you will see few trees. Look for the delightful waterfalls on the Allt Mor na h-Uamha and then step across the hurrying burn.

3 Stroll further along the path to cross Allt na h-Uamha on convenient boulders. Look upstream for more foaming waterfalls. As you follow the path the low-lying isle of Muck comes into view, with Beinn Airein standing prominent and square. Further on you pass, on the left, Lochan Dubh. Enjoy the grand views and then follow the path downhill to cross Allt-nam-Ba hurrying down the slopes of Beinn nan Stac. Look for a plummeting waterfall where the silvery burn hurtles over boulders and the side of a ravine in its ecstatic leap to reach the sea.

4 Follow the path as it climbs steadily, winding round the skirts of the mountain. Then the path comes close to the edge of high cliffs and care is required. Look for the green top of a stack, lower than the path. The way then moves inland, passing through bracken and steadily descending to the Dibidil River, which you ford. Continue ahead to the bothy at the foot of Glen Dibidil, where you will want to pause or descend to the shore.

5 Then go up the glen and cross the Dibidil River where it seems easiest. Then head on up the pathless rough vegetation using small animal paths to help you along. Towards the top of the glen follow a burn on the right into a small corrie, heading for the Bealach an Oir, the col to the right of Trollaval, between it and Askival. Look back for panoramic views down the glen and out to Eigg and Muck, with Ardnamurchan behind, and, on a clear day, Mull in the distance.

6 From the bealach, which is quite enclosed, go fairly steeply down the other side into Atlantic Corrie. This is a great wide sweep of a corrie running down from Askival and Hallival to the sea at Harris, halfway along Rum's south west coast. Keep to right across the head of the corrie, below the cliffs and boulder fields on the steep slopes of Askival but above the bogs of the corrie floor; the going is rough and rocky but not too difficult. Halfway across the corrie pick up a path which climbs gently and easily across the side of Hallival to the Bealach Bairc-mheall. Watch out for the burrows of the shearwaters here. You are unlikely to encounter the birds unless you go up on a dark night in late summer, when you may be treated to the sight and sound of hundreds of birds returning to their nests to feed their young.

7 The bealach is broad and sandy, with easy slopes leading up to Hallival on the right and Barkeval on the left. Descend a steep sandy slope on the far side down into Coire Dubh and soon cross a burn to join a good path down its west side. Go past the remains of a dam then, at a deer fence, go left to reach a gate. Beyond it, return to the riverbank and follow the delightful burn down past pools and rapids and another dam, built by Sir George Bullough to improve the water supply to the castle.

8 Enter the trees and continue, passing to the right of the generator house, to go through a gate and, still beside the burn, cross the lawn at the side of Kinloch Castle. Cross a stile, which gives access to the track by the castle.

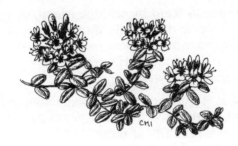

Thyme

Practicals

Type of walk: This is another long hard walk. The return over the mountains should not be attempted unless you are well equipped and quite experienced at finding your way across country. It should not be attempted in mist or high winds. There are several burns to be crossed and if these are in spate, you will have to return. If the weather deteriorates and heavy rain falls remember that the burns will be higher and much more difficult to cross.

Total Distance:	10 miles/16km
Time:	8 hours
Maps:	OS Explorer 397 / Landranger 39

31a

Kinloch River Trail, Rum

See walk 29 for details on reaching the island.

As you approach Rum by sea, the island shows its extreme ruggedness. It has a dozen fine mountains and much rough moorland. There are no metalled roads. Two stony tracks lead from Kinloch village, one to Harris and the other to Kilmory. There are several pony tracks.

The island of Rum was left to **George Bullough** by his father, John, a manufacturer of cotton mill equipment. John was a hard-working business man whose father had been a simple weaver. George, tall and good looking, became a cavalry officer. He later travelled the world in his early twenties in the family's steam-powered yacht. At the age of 27 he decided that the estate on Rum was just right for a gentleman, a place where he could entertain and dazzle his society friends.

Hallival from Kinloch Glen

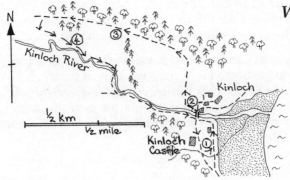

1 Leave Kinloch Castle and walk north along the path by the shore. Pass the former post office, the oldest inhabited building on Rum and once the kitchen of Kinloch House. Originally occupied by the laird of the island, Kinloch House was demolished after the castle was built. Go on past a small house in a clump of trees, the former dairy.

2 Cross the bridge over the Kinloch River and turn left through a gate to stroll a track shaded by willow, ash, oak and pine. Beyond the wooded area, turn right and follow a track up through pasture. Pass through a gate in the wall and bear left to walk through more woodland, passing the millionth planted tree on Rum. Go on to pass a long, very narrow plantation on the left, which stretches to the river.

3 Continue on, through the woodland, along beside the wall. Just before more straggly woodland, bear left through a gap in the

Curlew

121

wall. Descend to the side of the river. Here turn left and, using duckboarding over the wet areas, walk with the lovely river to your right, crossing two small streams on your way.

4 You might like to pause on a seat which carries a plaque saying that it was dedicated to a man who loved to watch birds. Stroll on over more duckboards to cross the river by a footbridge. Proceed along a wide track beside the hurrying water where it descends in pretty falls. Join another track and bear left to return to the castle.

Northern Eggar Moth

Practicals

Type of walk: A short enjoyable waymarked route, which might fit in with a day trip to the island – perhaps after a visit to the castle.

Total Distance: 2½ miles/4km
Time: 1½ hours
Maps: OS Explorer 397 / Landranger 39

Loch Scresort Trail, Rum

To reach the island, see walk 29.

An army of 300 builders and craftsmen worked for three years to construct and furnish the **castle at Kinloch** for George Bullough. The building, which cost £250,000 to complete, soon employed 100 servants. It had hydro-electric light, a telephone link to Newmarket racecourse so that George could check on his racehorses. The bathtub has to be seen to be believed. The ochestrion, a system of organ tubes, drums and cymbals and powered by an electric motor,'read' music from punched rolls of paper; it still plays. The castle is rose-coloured. It was built of red sandstone quarried at Annan in Dumfriesshire and shipped the 160 miles to Rum.

Limekiln

George married Monique Charrington, a French divorcee, in 1903 and soon received a knighthood. In 1957 Lady Monica sold the entire island estate including the castle to **Scottish Natural Heritage** for £ 23,000. It is now a National Nature Reserve. The reserve welcomes everyone but the island is not developed for tourism. It is primarily managed to maintain its outstanding natural heritage value and to encourage greater awareness of that value through education and quiet enjoyment, including walking.

1 From Kinloch Castle, turn right (south) and walk along the tree-lined avenue to the White House, which houses the Nature Reserve office. At the office take the left hand track, which skirts the bay, and pass a limekiln built in 1850. The woodland in this area was planted just before the castle was built. Continue on towards the stone-built pier, which dates from the mid-19 century. It stands on the edge of Loch Sresort, the only deep-water bay on the island.

2 Continue along the road towards the end of the village where the large building housing the primary school once doubled as the church. Turn right and climb the slope. At the top, turn left and walk on to take an arrowed path on the right. Stroll through the trees and out onto moorland. Look for the many small rowans and birches emerging from the low-growing vegetation now that sheep have been removed from the island (1957) and deer kept back behind deer fences. Press on into shady woodland and look left for a solitary grave, the burial place of a seaman from a cargo ship, who drowned in 1928. Several ruined cottages stand among trees where you might spot herons nesting.

3 Follow the path down onto a pebble beach overlooking Loch Scresort. Look across the sea to the Skye Cuillin, with the low-lying island of Soay in front. Then move into more woodland, where several aspen grow. Descend a rougher part of the track onto the pebbled shore of Carn-an-Dobhrain Bhig, meaning the cairn of the little otter. Here you might spot an otter. Go on along the path over moorland to the ruined village of Port-na-Caranean. Five crofters moved here from Skye in 1827 after the people of Rum were shipped to Nova Scotia in 1826. Now eiders nest among the ruins.

4 After a pause here, return by the same route.

Eiders

Practicals

Type of walk: A pleasing linear walk of moderate difficulty, involving some rock scrambling, which might fit into time spent on the island during a day trip. The instructions start from the castle.

Total Distance: 3½ miles/5.5km
Time: 2–3 hours
Maps: OS Explorer 397 / Landranger 39

32

Kinloch to Kilmory, Rum

To reach the island of Rum, see walk 29

The northern part of Rum, from Kilmory Glen to the Sound dividing the island from Skye is almost entirely moorland. Much of it is used for red deer research and, in the east, for experimental afforestation. There are quite large areas of woodland above the north shore that were planted relatively recently. The bird life is diverse and sea eagles have been re-introduced.

Stone Crusher

CM Isherwood

The **research taking place at Kilmory** is being done by Cambridge University. It is one of the longest running studies of large mammals in the world. It looks at breeding success, habitat use and the survival of red deer in the research area.

1 Start your day as for walk 29, leaving the trees behind as you pass through the tall gate in the deer fence. Look left as you go to see a stone crusher standing high on a rocky outcrop, once used to provide suitable sized stones for repairing the track. After two miles from the castle, the rough stony way divides. Here take the right branch and press on along an equally rough way. Pause, as you go, to enjoy a dramatic view of the Isle of Skye.

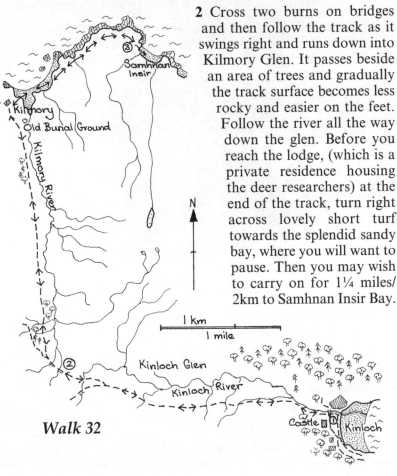

2 Cross two burns on bridges and then follow the track as it swings right and runs down into Kilmory Glen. It passes beside an area of trees and gradually the track surface becomes less rocky and easier on the feet. Follow the river all the way down the glen. Before you reach the lodge, (which is a private residence housing the deer researchers) at the end of the track, turn right across lovely short turf towards the splendid sandy bay, where you will want to pause. Then you may wish to carry on for 1¼ miles/ 2km to Samhnan Insir Bay.

Walk 32

If so continue on round the shore above rocks and low cliffs to come to another sandy bay, equally delightful and even more remote. Look for waders on the edge of the water: ringed plovers and oystercatchers, and at the right time of the year you might spot basking sharks off shore.

3 Return by the same route to Kilmory Bay. Then walk the track by the lodge and turn left to retrace your steps to Kinloch Castle.

Red Deer

Practicals

Type of walk: Two delightful bays are visited but this does involve rough track walking for most of the route. The scenery is wonderful.

Total Distance: 13 miles/21km
Time: 5–6 hours
Maps: OS Explorer 397 / Landranger 39

33

An Sgurr, Island of Eigg

The island lies 13 miles (21km) from the mainland port of Mallaig. It has one road, which runs north-south and divides in two at each end. Several times a week Caledonian MacBrayne's **passenger ferry** (tel 01687 462403) calls at the sturdy pier (grid ref 486838), where there is tearoom and restaurant, craft shop, information centre and a shop. To 'Get on-line' use www.calmac.co.uk. MV *Shearwater* also cruises to Eigg from Arisaig, providing a seven-day service for much of the year, weather permitting, with time ashore to explore. For information, tel 01687 450224.

From the mainland, **An Sgurr**, 1291ft/393m, Eigg's great pitchstone lava block, is seen dominating the island, towering over green pastures, heather moorland and the high platform of Beinn Bhuidhe. From neighbouring Rum and Muck, Eigg seems just a step over the sea.

An Sgurr

On June 12, 1997, conservationists, politicians, well wishers and residents of the island came together to unveil a plaque above the jetty, commemorating the purchase of the island. It took seven months to raise the £1.5 million to buy the island by **The Isle of Eigg Heritage Trust** from the last owner. The Trust includes representatives of the Eigg community, the Scottish Wildlife Trust and Highland Council who, altogether, now manage the island and aim to build a better future for it.

1 Leave the pier, pass the pier complex, and after 100yds/90m take the left fork where the road divides. Pass the 1997 'Independence Stone', ignore a dead end road on your left and go on through glorious woodland. Cross a cattle grid continue past a house on your left. Ignore the white wooden gates of The Lodge on your right, and the iron gate on your left. Follow the road as it winds its way up through trees. Then pass through a gate into open pasture. Stroll towards sturdy Galmisdale House, once an inn, at the top of the field. Carry on through a gate to the right of the dwelling to join the track beyond.

2 Turn left to walk the reinforced track coming in on your right. After 55yds/50m take the grassy path that climbs right, between bracken and heather. Go on climbing the good path and enjoy the magnificent views. Look up at the awesome pitchstone ridge of An Sgurr and then follow the path as it curves round the Nose of the Sgurr. Carry on along the north side of the majestic lump. Try your echo as you walk.

3 Three quarters of the way along the magnificent side of the Sgurr, follow the path as it turns south into a gully between high walls of pitchstone. On reaching a cairn, you need to scramble up the indistinct way, on the left, to join a clear path. Follow this enjoying, as you go, the grand view of the Isle of Muck, far below. Then pause to look down, immediately below, to the only visible building on

An Sgurr ←393m

N

½ km

½ mile

Galmisdale

Pier

Walk 33

130

Kestrel

the wide grassy plateau at Grulin. Once the area had two settlements, and it is possible to trace the foundations of many houses. In the far distance you can see the islands of Coll, Tiree and Mull, and the shoreline of Ardnamurchan. While here on this airy top you might find yourself on a level with a hovering kestrel.

4 Walk over the pitchstone pavement, keeping to the left of a small lochan. Go on, with care, over the cobbled top of An Sgurr and then, scramble, left, to the trig point. Here a great view awaits you, of the Cuillin of Rum, the Cuillin of Skye, and the Torridons. Then descend by the same route and retrace your steps to the pier.

Practicals

Type of walk: A delightful walk over generally good paths. Superb views.

Total Distance:	6 miles/9.7km
Time:	3–4 hours. If time is short because of transport, you could take a taxi (ask at the shop at the pier) to Galmisdale House and walk from there to the top of An Sgurr and back (2½ hours).
Maps:	OS Explorer 397 / Landranger 39

34

Cleadale and the Singing Sands, Eigg

To reach the island of Eigg, see walk 33.

This 12 miles/19 km walk will take 6–7 hours and can be completed if you are staying on the island. If you have climbed An Sgurr on another day, take the same route to its foot and then continue from the start of the pitchstone gully (point 3, walk 33).

As you pass **Loch nam Ban Mora**, look for its small island. This is believed to be a crannog, constructed and fortified by the Picts. They were small people and many could crowd on the island in times of trouble, keeping themselves warm with peat fires.

When you reach Camas Sgiotaig, **'Singing Sands Bay'**, scuff the sands when dry to make them sing. It is more of a squeak

Rum from Bay of Laig (Eigg)

than a song: the pressure of your boots forces out air trapped between the quartz grains.

1 After you have walked to the summit of An Sgurr (see walk 33) and have returned to the foot of the pitchstone gully, or you have ignored the summit, head slightly west of north. Keep along a sheep trod to the north east (right) side of Loch nam Ban Mora with its small island. Edge along the shore or through the heather above. Here on the little loch you might spot a pair of red-throated divers. Bear half right at the end of the loch to join a path that comes close to the west (left) side of the next loch, Loch Caol na Cora-bheinne. Stroll along the shore as it stretches below Cora-bheinn, a wonderful exposure of columnar rock.

2 Then begin to descend, due north, soon to come to the right side of the narrow burn, Abhainn Gleann Charadail. Keep close to the hurrying water, edged with narrow strips of grass, moving from one side to the other of the narrow rivulet to find the easiest way to tackle this challenging part of the walk. Make full use of sheep trods. Great areas of heather, with an understorey of sphagnum, stretch away to the hills beyond the grassy strip. Continue down Gleann Charadail.

Walk 34

3 Keep well above an attractive waterfall, as do the sheep. Then the heather becomes shorter and a narrow path leads on along a low ridge. Stay on this and follow the contours round above an extensive area of willow woodland. While remaining on high-level ground, cross the burn at the point just before the stream begins to descend into a steep-sided gorge.

4 Beyond, stride a much clearer path to pass through a large circle of short bracken, with circles of stones nearby, possibly ruined huts (shielings). The path passes through a grassy gully and as you climb out of this you can see Cleadale, and the extensive afforestation in the centre of the island. And then the glorious Bay of Laig, with its blue, blue water rolling in over golden sand comes into view.

5 Go on until you reach a fence. Follow it, left, to join a path zig-zagging steeply down to Laig, once a largish settlement. You may wish to cut your walk short here. If so take the path that goes off right, past the ruins of the old Laig township, near the loch of the giant's footstep, Loch an Fhiantaiche. The way continues up through a fine gorge with magnificent waterfalls, to join the road, where you turn right to return.

6 To continue with this walk, join the track that passes right of a farmhouse and continue by a stile to the glorious sands, where cattle paddle and, further along, in summer, families swim. Leave

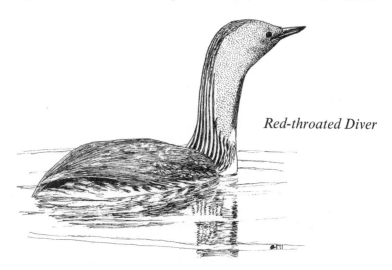

Red-throated Diver

the bay by a track that leads to the Roman Catholic church, which you might wish to visit. Then walk on along the shallow cliffs of sculptured sandstone, with dykes of dolerite striking seaward. Enjoy a dramatic view of Rum.

7 As you near Singing Sands Bay, keep to the path inside the fence along the higher cliffs, the only safe way down to the shore. Immediately left of the sands is a natural arch and a canyon, a great place for children to explore. After time spent on the sands, return to the top of the cliffs by the same path and then strike diagonally left over rough pasture in the direction of the obvious pinnacle (God's Finger) away on Beinn Bhuidhe. At the fence, follow it right to join a wide fenced way to the left of a bungalow.

8 Join the road and walk right. Just past the junction of roads is Cleadale Crafts, a renovated crofthouse, where you can get a cup of tea. Climb the hill to Bealach Clithe and walk on to pass a path, coming in on your right. This is where the short cut from Laig, joins the 'main' road.

9 Walk on along the quiet narrow road as it continues through the island, passing the shop and post office on its way. Beyond the school, keep on the right branch of the road, to continue to the pier.

Practicals

Type of walk: Long and challenging with lots of rewards along the way.

Total Distances:	12 miles/19km or, if you shorten it at Laig and do not climb An Sgurr, 7½ miles/12km.
Time:	6–7 hours or 4 hours
Maps:	OS Explorer 397 / Landranger 39

35

Kildonan, Eigg

See walk 33 for details of transport to the island of Eigg.

The site of the **Iron Age fort** is just a depression, bordered with stones. A smaller stone circle lies beside it. St Donan, who introduced Christianity to Eigg, is thought to have occupied the fort while monks built a wooden church on the hill, on the site of the present graveyard.

1 Leave the pier by the only road and follow it as it turns right to skirt Galmisdale Bay. To the left stands deciduous woodland and in the ditch below the road, in summer, water avens grow, shading from gold to deep pink. Just beyond Shore Cottage, take the track leading right. Look right to see the disused Clanranald

Clanranald Harbour, Eigg

Pier, left high and dry when the tide ebbs and often under water at high tide. Stroll on along the track, shaded by hazel, wych elm, ash and oak. Step (or wade if necessary) across the Allt Eas Chuthain and head for a wooden beach hut. Then carry on, north east, over pasture. Continue ahead to a gap in the wall. (Ignore the gate in the fence on the left.)

Walk 35

2 Keep to the path that runs parallel with the bracken to your right. Where the way divides, take the right branch that continues up the slope. Step across the next stream and walk on, with bracken and the fenced cliff to your right. Climb to the fence post at the highest point and then go ahead for a 100yds/92m, with care, and through a convenient gap on your right. Beyond, walk circumspectly close to the cliff edge, steadily descending into hazel woodland. Pass through a small gate and saunter on. Eiders and sandpipers call from the bay, Poll nam Partan, below. Follow the path as it continues below a cliff of magnificent columns to the road.

Common Sandpiper

3 Turn right and go on past the old cornmill with the remains of its huge waterwheel. Stride on, keeping to the right of Kildonan guesthouse, and walk out to the site of the Iron-Age fort. Then leave the fort and return past the farm. Take the upper of two tracks to visit the ruined church and graveyard. There is a cross of schist (probably 15 century) by the graves. It has lost its cross head, which was a replacement, and stands at the

foot of the shaft. The new graveyard lies close by. Beyond, is the picturesque roofless church, yellowed with lichen and overgrown with weeds.

4 Return to the pier by the same route or, at low tide, cross the sands of Kildonan Bay, but expect to get wet feet.

Ringed Plovers

Practicals

Type of walk: Generally easy walking but strong footwear required. Wherever you take a summer walk on Eigg you will be rewarded by a plethora of wild flowers, wonderful woodlands and many birds. You might even spot otters at play.

Total Distance: 3 miles/5km
Time: 2 hours
Maps: OS Explorer 397 / Landranger 39

36

Massacre Cave and Cathedral, Eigg

To reach the island of Eigg, see walk 33.

Cathedral Cave, a huge lofty cavern, where drops of water descend in a curtain, was used for illicit services after the Reformation, 1745, when Roman Catholicism was banned. If the tide is right, you might be able to sit on the rocks and watch an otter at play, but the entrance to the cave can be under water at high tide.

In **Massacre Cave**, which has a low 20 ft/6m narrow entrance passage before opening out into a large cavern, more than 390 MacDonalds perished. In 1577 all the people of Eigg, men, women and children, were hiding in the cave from the MacLeods of Skye who were bent on retribution for a

Cathedral Cave

139

Walk 36

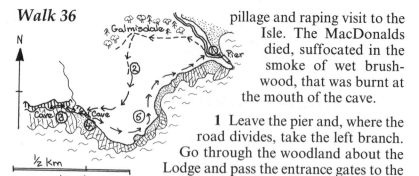

pillage and raping visit to the Isle. The MacDonalds died, suffocated in the smoke of wet brushwood, that was burnt at the mouth of the cave.

1 Leave the pier and, where the road divides, take the left branch. Go through the woodland about the Lodge and pass the entrance gates to the estate on your right. Stroll on a little to take, on the left, a metal gate and walk on along a track. Look to the right of the way for an old well. Carry on past Craigard Cottage on a grassy path. At the following slight rise, leave the path as it swings off right and follow a sheep track going straight ahead.

2 Press on, keeping parallel with the cliff edge but about 100yds/90m inland. Cross a stile and descend the stepped zigzag track, which can be slippery and difficult after rain, down towards the shore, beside the burn. A grassy path right, westwards, continues along the skirt of the great cliffs, steadily dropping to the shore. Then after a little scrambling you reach the entrance to Cathedral Cave. Remember that it is tidal. If you get cut off remain where you are until the tide recedes. Do not climb the cliffs as they are dangerously crumbly.

Otters

140

3 Return along the narrow path to the burn and then descend another narrow path, eastwards (left) to the shore. Walk on a few steps and look up above the gently-sloping greensward to see a low narrow opening. This is the entrance to Massacre Cave.

4 Return to the pier by your outward route or climb back up beside the burn and return along the cliffs. To do the latter, ignore your approach route along the sheep trod and continue on, parallel with the sea, through bracken. Then follow the path as it swings inland for a few yards. Use a plank bridge to cross a small stream that flows through a small ravine, lush with oak, willow and flags.

5 A little way along, watch for the place where the track drops right, through bracken, and then continues in the same general direction, below willow scrub to a stile. Walk on a few yards and then swing right to descend a rough stony way that drops towards the sea. It is easy to miss this turn when the bracken is high. It lies just beyond mixed woodland that hugs a huge bluff of rock. From here the way, sometimes wet, continues over meadows to the pier.

Willow

Practicals

Type of walk: Fairly easy walking. Care needs to be taken on the path down the cliffs. Choose a good day to enjoy the seashore. Check times of tides.

Total Distance: 2 miles/3.4km
Time: 2 hours
Maps: OS Explorer 397 / Landranger 39

37

Circular walk around the coast of the island of Canna

The Caledonian MacBrayne ferry from Mallaig (tel: 01687 46 2403 for details, or visit www.calmac.co.uk) calls at Canna on its way to the other Small Isles. It visits several days of the week and sometimes stays for an hour at the deep-water pier, grid ref 278051, where there is a fine teashop.

Canna is a green island with rocky outcrops and very high cliffs. In 1981, it was given to the National Trust for Scotland (NTS) by the late Dr and Mrs J.L Campbell of Canna House. The island lies north-west of Rum, Eigg and Muck and to the south-west of Skye. The island has almost no metalled roads but provides much pleasing walking.

View, almost at the start of the walk, a stack named **Prison Rock**, An Coroghon. Look high up to see a tiny stone hut, called a castle on the Ordnance Survey map. It was here, in about 1666, a chief of the Clanranald imprisoned his wife to prevent her seeing her lover, a MacLeod of Skye.

Prison Rock

The NTS asks that you do not climb to the little building; the very steep way up is badly eroded and very dangerous.

Compass Hill is so named because the iron in the rock distorted the compasses of ships. Place your compass on several outcrops and find out for yourself.

Look out for the two **souterrains**. These are Bronze-age subterranean earth houses, perhaps used for storage or shelter. The entrance in both has a stone lintel. You can just about wriggle inside.

From a shallow cliff look down to see an arrangement of boulders that is long and narrow and faces north-west. This is known as a **Viking grave** and because of its shape it may have contained a boat. It is known locally as the grave of the King of Norway.

The **nunnery** used to house Irish women who sailed in skin-covered boats to live on Canna, and hence avoid all worldly temptations.

1 From the pier walk along a metalled track past the Presbyterian church. Beyond, turn right up a walled track to take the gate on the left, opposite a barn. Walk along the edge of the pasture. Follow the fence as it edges a small wood. Pass through the next gate and walk on to a rocky shore to view Prison Rock. Return through the last gate and turn right. Climb beside the fence on your right, go through the next gate and continue. Where the trees cease, look left to view groups of stones, all that remains of

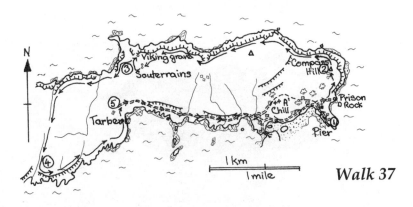

Walk 37

143

several shielings (shepherds' huts). Then climb on to Compass Hill.

2 Head on north and then west along the pasture of the coast, keeping well away from the sheer cliff edges and intruding ravines. Follow sheep trods that take you the easiest way. Climb a stile over a fence. Pause here to look across the sea to the Skye Cuillin. Follow the good trods through heather, avoiding wet areas flagged with cotton grass, until you reach a protective fence on your right, which also protects the sheep from the edge of the immensely steep cliffs. Walk inland on narrow paths along the upper reaches of steep-sided ravines to a point where it is easy and safe to cross. Then the way steadily descends. As you go look left to see a parallel wall and descend towards it. Walk beside it (west) and then a little left (south) inland. Look for a south-facing slope close to the wall to see the souterrains. Cross the wall to continue west and pass, on a green sward, the stone remnants of an Iron Age settlement.

3 Then swing right, back towards the cliffs, and follow a clear path that leads to the edge of a shallow cliff, overlooking an apron of low-lying land. From here you can see the 'Viking grave'. Continue westwards, keeping to the landward side of steep crags edging more cliffs. Then follow a sheep trod down to pass through a gate to walk around Thairbearnais Bay. At the far side of the bay, and a few steps inland, climb the fence by a sturdy hurdle. Then bear right to walk beside the fence towards the sea cliffs once more. Carry on for ½ mile/1km to a fence that edges a river, the Allt na Criche Tuatha. Follow this left for ¾ mile/1.4km to cross the island north to south.

Manx Shearwaters gathering offshore

4 Towards the end of the fence, bear left to walk east along the southern side of Canna. After about a mile pass through a gate in the low wall. Beyond this, look over the fenced cliff edge and you will see the site of an ancient fort. Go on, circumspectly, along the cliffs. Where you begin to descend, look down the cliffs again to see, on a terrace far below, the ruins of a nunnery. (Do not attempt to descend.) Then walk on, following the coastline as it goes along the western side of Tarbert Bay to Tarbert, a ruined crofthouse with a large barn.

5 Join the gated track and walk right. After nearly two miles, with grand views all the way, take the left branch at the Y-junction to return to the pier. If you walk this way in late evening, you stand a chance of seeing Manx shearwaters on the wing.

Greylag Geese

Practicals

Type of walk: This is a long, delightful walk especially if you choose a good day when there is little wind. It is suitable for seasoned fell walkers who are staying on the island.

Total Distance: 10 miles/16km
Time: 6–7 hours
Maps: OS Explorer 397 / Landranger 39

38

A short walk on Canna or a longer walk taking in the island of Sanday

See details of how to reach Canna in the previous walk.

Sanday projects east from Canna like a long arm and gives good shelter to the natural deep harbour and the pier. Between Canna and Sanday the water drains out on the ebb, leaving just a trickle at the west end. The road from the pier, suitable for vehicles, ends at a foot-bridge, frequently washed away (last time in 2004) but first built by the parish council in 1905. It links the two islands. Beyond the footbridge a road continues and at low tide vehicles cross the channel to gain access to it, to reach the houses and school on Sanday.

St Edward's, the striking Roman Catholic church on Sanday, is no longer used. Go inside the listed building, which was constructed in 1885, and look for the carved mouse, trademark of the Thompson family of woodcarvers, from Kilburn in Yorkshire.

Old Roman Catholic Church, Sanday

1 Walk the road from the pier to pass, on your right, the Presbyterian church. Where the track turns left, walk a path that goes ahead to continue beside the east wall of Canna House. Follow the path as it makes a tight zigzag beneath trees. Pass through a metal gate and continue ahead, with a wall to your left and a fuchsia hedge to your right, to pass in front of a house called Tighard. Follow the path through pleasing woodland. Go on into a pasture and follow the wall on your left. Pass through a gate in the wall.

2 Continue on to go over the site of a ruined village, razed in the evictions of 1850, to view a standing stone, with a small hole in it. Some say it was a punishment stone, others that it might have been used as a calendar. Head on to see a Celtic cross, with one arm missing. Go on over a stile. Carry on beside a planting of deciduous trees to join a cart track. Follow it to pass a small building, used as the Roman Catholic church, to join the main track from the pier. For a short walk, turn left to return for the ferry.

Celtic Cross, Canna

147

3 To continue with the longer walk, turn right. Follow the road where it swings left and then cross the footbridge. Go on past several houses and the little school – one room in the teacher's house. Continue to a pasture and take a gently rising path away from the shore. Walk on toward the Roman Catholic church and perhaps visit it.

4 Then leave the church by a gate in the wall and walk in a clockwise direction above the shoreline. There are no footpaths from now on, but tractor wheel marks and sheep tracks make walking easier. Head on slightly right to pass through a gate in the boundary wall ahead of you. Then bear left to regain the shallow sea cliffs and continue around the bay, Camas Stianabhaig. Follow the headland round. As you breast a slope, the huge cliffs of Rum come into view and then Sanday's sturdy automatic light. Look for huge stacks where you might spot puffins and fulmars.

5 Wind on round the lovely high-level southern coastline where, in spring, spring squill shades the grass to blue. At a fence, follow it left to cross a gully and then climb the next mound, the site of an Iron Age fort. You can just discern a circle of stones around a depression. Leave the fort by the way you climbed up and go on. Here look for white burnet roses above the Bay of Suileabhaig. Walk on past a wet area on your right, where struggling alders, willows and conifers have been fenced.

6 Pass through the gate in the wall (taken earlier) and turn left to

Puffins

go on along high cliffs. Go through the gap in the next wall and walk on. Step across a deepish ditch using a stone causeway, then keep to higher ground to the right. When a wooden house comes into view, walk right to a gate. Beyond, drop down, left, towards the shore, passing through another gate. Join the road taken earlier and follow this, left, to cross the footbridge. Walk on and then bear right to return to the pier.

Spring Squill

Practicals

Type of walk: A pleasing walk with few footpaths. Dramatic views for much of the way.

Total Distances:	Short walk 2 miles/3.2km; long walk 6½ miles/10.5km
Time:	1 hour or 3 hours.
Terrain:	Generally easy walking but can be wet underfoot. It will be enjoyed by seasoned fell walkers.
Maps:	OS Explorer 397 / Landranger 39

39

Beinn Airein and Horse Island, Muck

Caledonian MacBrayne run a passenger ferry from Mallaig to Port Mor on the island of Muck. For details tel: 01687 462403.

Muck, with a population of 30, is a delightful, peaceful, friendly island, which lies three miles off Eigg and measures two miles by one. It has hay meadows, cattle pastures, moorland and a steepish hill, Beinn Airein (451ft/146m), which has high cliffs. It has a wonderful broken shoreline. Visitors can walk anywhere on the island, except in private gardens and buildings.

The island is owned by the **MacEwen** family who farm it. There is also a good craft shop, the crafts mainly being made on the island or by friends. The tearoom and restaurant provide home-baked and fresh-from-the-oven food. On the island there is a variety of accommodation including a small hotel, B&B, bunkhouse, self catering cottages and even a yurt.

Old Crofthouse, Muck

The island has one road, which runs from the pier to the farm at Gallanach, situated on the north coast of the island. Close by is **Horse Island**, reached on foot at low tide. In coves around the little island grey seals haul out on rocks and in October a dozen pups maybe born here.

1 Walk from the pier to pass a stone house. This was once used as a salt store and upstairs was the island's first school. Then go on to pass the craft shop and the tearoom and restaurant. The prominent building behind is today's school and the community hall. Continue to the graveyard, on the left, and climb to the stone-built memorial, commemorating three people who drowned near Horse Island. Above the graveyard is the site of the ruined village of Keil, which was deserted in 1828, the time of the Clearances.

2 Climb straight uphill and turn left to Caisteal an Duin Bhain, a rock, once fortified, on the promontory overlooking Port Mor. Head on round towards inland cliffs, to the left of a small plantation of mixed conifers. Use helpful sheep trods to reach the cairn on Fionn-aird, from where there is a spectacular view. Stroll along the cliffs that curve round a dramatic bay of black basalt boulders and crags. Cross the fence and go on above the

Grey Seals

bay of Fang Mor. Pass through a gate and then strike uphill along a track.

3 At the wall walk, right, to its north end, to pass through a gate by a pleasing stone sheepfold. Keep by the fence, ignore the stile over it, and follow the fence until you can pass through a gate on your right to walk inside the fence, now on your left. Continue steeply uphill over grass, the fence still edging the sheer cliffs to your left. Where the fence ends at a flaring cliff, take a stony trod up the slope, on the right, to reach the cairn on Beinn Airein. On a good day you can see Coll, Tiree, the Treshnish Isles, Iona, Mull, the Mainland, Skye, Eigg, Rum, Canna, South Uist, Barra, Vatersay and Eriskay. The summit cliffs drop sheer almost to the sea at Camas Mor, the island's SSSI, and on these cliffs nest many seabirds.

4 Leave by the route taken to the top and at the fence climb the good stile and head on over the pasture, left, to a gate in the corner. Go on ahead, with a fence to the left and then when it ceases continue to follow an indistinct narrow path that has helpful planks and stones to aid you over the wet patches of Aird nan Uan. Aim for the crofthouse following the contours round an old dyke. The tiny listed building has been restored and has a turf roof. Then go on over boggy ground to reach a small bay with a beach composed entirely of small sea shells, where you will want to linger.

5 Return to the crofthouse and walk on to the next little bay to pass through a gate in a derelict stone wall. Ahead on the site of a Bronze-Age burial circle, stand stones commemorating MacEwens buried here. Beyond is the way to Horse Island.

Climb onto Lamb Island first and then scramble over seaweed-covered rocks. This can only be attempted at low water at spring tides. (Ask at Gallanach for exact times).

6 Wind on round the low cliffs overlooking Gallanach Bay. Seals call mournfully from the shallow water below. Don't miss the way down by a cottage and then descend the path to the road to return to the pier.

Turnstones

Practicals

Type of walk: A very pleasing walk mainly over paths and a mile on a narrow road. Expect some wet parts. Take care on the high cliffs.

Total Distance:	5¼ miles/8.5km
Time:	You could spend all day on this walk but if you are returning to the Mainland on the same day you should turn back and retrace your steps in good time to catch the ferry.
Maps:	OS Explorer 397 / Landranger 39

40

Circular walk round the east end of Muck

See walk 39 for reaching the island.

Electricity did not reach Muck until 1970, when one Lister diesel generator was connected to all the houses at Port Mor and another to the farmhouse and buildings at Gallanach. The hissing Tilley lamps, which for the previous 25 years had illuminated the island's homes, were packed away, and soon almost every house had a freezer and a washing machine.

In 1992 an ambitious plan was mooted: to connect every house to a 60KVA **wind generator** situated on the summit of Carn Dearg. For the windless days a central diesel generator was connected to the system. This provides 10 hours of guaranteed power on calm days.

Harbour, Muck

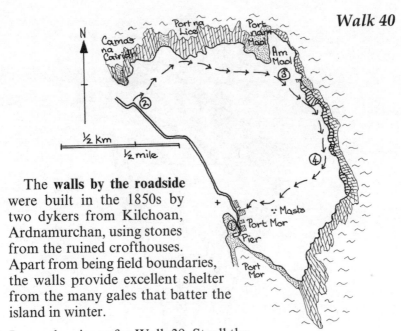

The **walls by the roadside** were built in the 1850s by two dykers from Kilchoan, Ardnamurchan, using stones from the ruined crofthouses. Apart from being field boundaries, the walls provide excellent shelter from the many gales that batter the island in winter.

1 Leave the pier as for Walk 39. Stroll the quiet road for just under a mile to where, at a sharp corner, the road comes close to the sandy shore of Camas na Cairidh. Leave the road, right, to pass through a gateless gap in the wall. Stroll to the top right corner to go through a second gate. Continue left over the ridge with the cliff on the left. Cross the second fence, where there are no barbs. Walk on, edging a hay meadow on its seaward side. Overhead common gulls call. Cross the next wall by keeping along the shore. Go on over rough pastures, from where you can see Grulin on Eigg. Keep left of high ground ahead and left of a fence.

Common Gull

155

Bog Bean

2 Pass through a gate by a sheep pen and walk on by a small lochan, in summer almost overgrown by bog bean. Go round the next bay to pass a ruined building. Cross a deep ditch, which requires a large step, or keep on the shore if this presents difficulties. Walk on along a sheep trod, bearing right and following the contours around a hillock. Pass through a turf and stone dyke and go on along the trod, keeping above a very wet area. Here you can still see the outlines of lazybeds. This area was once under intensive cultivation. Continue to a gate in a fence where you are asked to 'Keep it shut'.

3 Proceed along the contours, keeping above another wet area, where ragged robin, flags, bog myrtle, reeds and orchids grow.

Step across a ditch (easier this time) and follow the trod around the fence. When the radio masts come into view, head towards them, picking the driest way. Join a wide reinforced track to the site of the wind generator. From here drop down the slope towards the houses around the pier, keeping left of a small clump of conifers, the school and community hall. Walk on to join the road to the pier.

Eigg from Muck

Practicals

Type of walk: This lovely coastal walk can be a wet underfoot in parts. There are no footpaths to follow.

Total Distance:	2½ miles/4km
Time:	1½ hours
Terrain:	Easy walking but strong footwear required.
Maps:	OS Explorer 397 / Landranger 39

Clan Walks

A series of walks described by Mary Welsh, covering some of the most popular holiday areas in the Scottish Highlands and Islands.

Titles published so far include:

1. 44 WALKS ON THE ISLE OF ARRAN
2. WALKING THE ISLE OF SKYE
3. WALKING WESTER ROSS
4. WALKS IN PERTHSHIRE
5. WALKING THE WESTERN ISLES
6. WALKING ORKNEY
7. WALKING SHETLAND
8. WALKING THE ISLES OF ISLAY, JURA AND COLONSAY
9. WALKING GLENFINNAN: THE ROAD TO THE ISLES
10. WALKS ON TIREE, COLL, COLONSAY AND A TASTE OF MULL
11. WALKING DUMFRIES AND GALLOWAY
12. WALKING ARGYLL AND BUTE
13. WALKING DEESIDE, DONSIDE AND ANGUS
14. WALKING THE TROSSACHS, LOCH LOMONDSIDE AND THE CAMPSIE FELLS
15. WALKING GLENCOE, LOCHABER AND THE GREAT GLEN

OTHER TITLES IN PREPARATION

Books in this series can be ordered through booksellers anywhere. In the event of difficulty write to
Clan Books, The Cross, DOUNE, FK16 6BE, Scotland.